Calculated Risk

A Master Plan for Common Stocks

"Take calculated risk—that is quite different from being rash"

George S. Patton

Calculated Risk
A Master Plan for Common Stocks

ROBERT M. SHARP

DOW JONES-IRWIN
Homewood, Illinois 60430

This publication is designed to provide accurate and
authoritative information in regard to the subject matter
covered. It is sold with the understanding that the
publisher is not engaged in rendering legal, accounting, or
other professional service. If legal advice or other expert
assistance is required, the services of a competent
professional person should be sought.

*From a Declaration of Principles jointly adopted by a Committee
of the American Bar Association and a Committee of Publishers.*

ISBN 0-87094-761-3

Library of Congress Catalog Card No. 85–52400

Printed in the United States of America

1 2 3 4 5 6 7 8 9 0 BC 3 2 1 0 9 8 7 6

To. My parents, aged 85, who know about perseverance,
My ever young wife, who is always supportive and
My three children in college, who provided the incentive

In 1966 a savings and loan bankruptcy closed the doors on my life savings of $11,567.22. The money had been carefully saved for nearly 20 years and all that escaped was $2,246.00 in common stock. It was a devastating experience! My father told me about the banking holiday of 1933, but nothing makes a point like personal experience.

That is what this book is all about—personal experience and probability. My conservative methods had brought me full circle and taught me that there is no such thing as a risk-free investment. That knowledge transformed me from a "saver" to a "player." I became a more aggressive investor with liberal use of margin. In 1982 my goals were met and I retired on the proceeds of the $2,246 that survived 1966.

Stock market speculation is a probability science—like weather forecasting—and some failure is certain. The object is to find favorable situations and play these consistently enough for the statistical laws to effect a net profit. There is an art to stock selection; but it is science that produces a proper payoff.

As part of that science, this book introduces six powerful new, mathematically based ideas and reduces each to rules and arithmetic. Computer assistance is included, but is not essential to the strategy.

I've analyzed my performance to tell you what works, what doesn't, and why. If you're disciplined enough to incorporate the principles into your investment practice, then you can join me in "shaking the money tree."

Robert M. Sharp

 *Acknowledgment*

In preparing this book, I owe thanks to F. Leigh Hales, who provided a forum for my seminars, encouraged the book project, made useful suggestions and supplied the word processing capability. Fellow college administrator, teacher, student, neighbor, agent without purse—friend: Leigh is all of this and more!

Contents

CHAPTER 1

Planning Perspective

Luck is infatuated with the efficient.
—*Persian Proverb*

Bernard Baruch, the great investor of the early 20th century, once commented on the stock market:

> If you are ready to give up everything else to study the whole history and background of the market and all the principal companies whose stocks are on the board as carefully as a medical student studies anatomy—if you can do all that, and, in addition, you have the cool nerves of a great gambler, the sixth sense of a clairvoyant, and the courage of a lion, you have a ghost of a chance![1]

Investors are attracted to the securities markets because of the liquidity and potential for significant gain. If you're after a quick profit, then you're likely to be disappointed. The market is unpredictable and requires a long-term commitment to average out the successes and failures. Most people quit after the first loss, and very few approach the market with a plan in hand that allows for—and expects—setbacks. The old adage "If you fail to plan, then you plan to fail" has a loud ring of truth for investors.

The subject is planning: a "motherhood" topic heartily endorsed but rarely discussed by market strategists.

Planning should be accomplished in an objective, rational environment, with realistic appraisal of resources and skills, long before the battle for investment survival begins. The master carpenter doesn't attempt to build a house without detailed plans, and neither should the investor try to build a fortune without the

---

[1]Herbert V. Prochnow, *The Complete Toastmaster* (New York: Prentice-Hall, 1960).

framework of reasonable goals, adequate assets, and a timetable of events that can be monitored and redirected as needed.

Planning starts with a vision of what is needed or wanted, and then a step-by-step process of how to get there evolves. The more ambitious the plan, the more risk that has to be accepted and consequently the more probability of failures. Accepting risk means that you look at the worst possible situation, determine if you could accept that, guard against it happening, and then proceed full speed toward your goal. Decide in advance what is to be done under all circumstances and then do it when the occasion demands.

As part of the planning process, you must sort out the important factors, discarding the trivial, applying a degree of objectivity that many people don't possess. This lack of objectivity is demonstrated by the professional securities analyst. He is submerged in so much material that the truly important things aren't weighted heavily enough in his recommendations—a case of not seeing the forest because of the trees.

The successful person sets goals, solves problems, and confidently takes risks after laying out the worst consequences beforehand. In short, he or she plans!

Later we will study the mechanics of buying and selling, building portfolios, and managing money. But before we rush into the trees, let's take a good look at the forest from a planning perspective.

UTILITY OF WEALTH

Utility is usefulness or the power to satisfy. How satisfying would it be to have an additional unit of wealth? Each of us must answer this in terms of the risk that we are willing to bear in the quest for more wealth. Epicurus said that "wealth consists not in having great possessions, but in having few wants." The fact that you're studying the stock market implies dissatisfaction with your current accumulation and indicates that you are looking toward more speculative ventures to increase wealth. Mark Twain said, "There are two times in a man's life when he should not speculate. When he can't afford it—and when he can!" You had better be certain that what you're seeking is worth risking what you now have. Figure 1–1 shows the effect of wealth on its utility to the owner as additional units are added. When you have little or no wealth at all, any accumulation is desirable, and each additional unit is

FIGURE 1–1 The Utility of Wealth

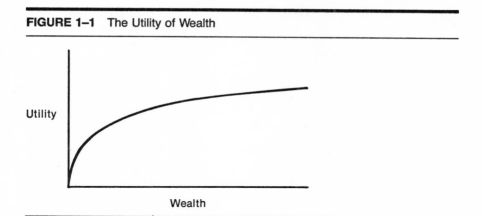

greatly satisfying. As the wealth continues to accumulate, at some point your needs are fulfilled, and there is less satisfaction from additional accumulation. That means you're on top of the curve, where very little pleasure is derived from additional hoarding. My kids reflect this state when they refuse $5 to mow the lawn.

Sometimes people reach a state of satisfaction and then slowly slip back down the incline. Hence the following true story:

A few years ago a casino in Las Vegas received a call asking if the house would allow a onetime bet of up to $500,000. The management considered and agreed to conduct a scheduled game for the caller. At the appointed time, a taxi deposited a man with a suitcase at the casino door. The suitcase containing $420,000 was checked in by the cashier and a single chip was issued. The game was played, and our man won. After cashing in his two special chips, he started for the door with a significantly heavier case. The manager's curiosity got the better of him; intercepting the winner, he asked what had compelled the man to risk that much money on a single play in the casino. The man answered: "It got so that money wasn't worth a damn to me, so I decided I had to double it or lose it!" Here was a man obviously backsliding on the utility-of-wealth curve.

Often the market won't deliver wealth according to the schedule you've set for it, and you have to ask yourself a very simple question: Will I be better off to take the remaining funds and either spend them on a luxury or deposit them against some future emergency, or is it worth trying again even if I should further diminish the wealth? In 1974 I recited this litany on a regular basis, and the answer was always, "Keep at it." Since I've satisfied my goals and have more at risk now, I'm sure the answer would be different the next time. I'm happily perched on top of my curve. You are the one to decide where you are located on yours.

THE ASSET PYRAMID

Having concluded that more wealth would be useful, it must be determined how much of our personal assets should be directed toward that quest. If we were to place everything in a pile, we might have a better perspective on what we are willing to put at risk. What we are about to do is isolate a portion of our assets as seed for speculation. It can be called investing, if that calms your emotions; but make no doubt about it, we are talking about speculation in the purest sense of the word. Investing involves a more or less specific return on a stable principal. Speculation has a less certain outcome. But then, all life is a speculation, is it not?

If we organize our assets into three categories, we'll have a better idea of how to approach the stock market. In the first category is survival possessions. This would include insurance, home equity, real estate, annuities, checking accounts, vehicles, household goods, college funds, retirement plans, possibly some commodities such as gold or collectibles such as stamps.

The first observation would be that the total would be inadequate for long-term survival. You must have some less tangible assets such as education, job skills and good health. If your determination is that you could survive less than a year on net worth, then something must be done about it. There are three possibilities:

1. You can concentrate on the saving process to lengthen the survival period. For most people, an entire life spent toward this goal is a failure, as demonstrated by dependence on social security. The normal accumulation process rarely provides independent wealth.

2. You can work on the less tangible assets. Expand your education and skills and the talents of your family. Promote your health to ensure a longer earning period.

3. The most radical approach would be to liquidate some of the hard assets to provide a fund for more active investment. This might mean sale of collectibles or surrender of insurance policies for cash after usefulness has diminished. What good is

life insurance on nonearning members of the family? In the case of the principal breadwinner, term insurance is the only sensible policy. Any savings or annuity plan is less preferable than the individual retirement accounts (IRAs), to realize the significant tax savings.

Regardless of your approach, you should review your assets and see what could be isolated and turned into cash for speculation without damaging the current level of survival. Sort out those to be turned into cash and put to work, and we'll deal with that fund later.

Next, look at income-producing assets (the second category). This would be any savings accounts, stocks and bonds, loans or mortgages held, business investments, profit sharing, and so forth. Are the yields adequate under *average* forseeable inflation and interest rates? If the rates are fixed and inflexible, is there any way the return can be upgraded without significant loss of principal? Does the total yield create a secure and adequate source of income for you in the future? Separate out those that aren't paying their way and turn these into cash.

Place the income-producing assets on top of the survival assets and then the assets converted to cash (the third category) on top of that, and you have the pyramid of Figure 1–2. The depth of each layer depends on your responsibilities, time in life, and comfort zone. Most of us never get past the first layer. Those who do, often skip the second layer to build a two-story pyramid of survival and speculation. Young people with job skills or college educations and no family responsibilities may have a pyramid of pure speculation. You can be the architect of your own structure.

Whatever shape your building takes, future expansion should come from the top as the speculative assets spill over, trickling into the lower levels. The top level is subject to continual revamping and will grow and diminish with the market cycles. Remember that a storm could blow it away at any time, and that should influence your expansion of the foundation.

The isolated cash to be used for speculation should be at least $4,000. If you don't have that amount, then place your bookmark here; and you may be excused to go save or borrow it. I can't tell you how to multiply zero by any other number and get anything but zero! Amounts less than $4,000 aren't practical to diversify, and the commissions will be exorbitant. Most advisers will tell you to stay out of the markets with less than $10,000, and some rec-

FIGURE 1–2 The Asset Pyramid

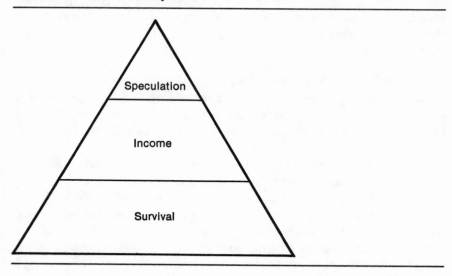

ommend $100,000. Obviously this is impractical advice! I began with less than $4,000, but commissions were easier then and my first ventures made money. The practical thing is to have enough of a stake to stay in the game when adversity is encountered.

MAXIM 1–1   Secure a minimum stake of $4,000 before speculating in stocks.

There is a handy little relationship between interest rates and the time it takes to double money. It is called the rule of 72. If you divide 72 by the interest rate, the result is the number of years required to double the principal. An interest rate of 6 percent would require 12 years to double the principal (72 ÷ 6 = 12). Assuming that we could produce a 25 percent annual rate of return, the money would double in slightly less than three years (72 ÷ 25 = 2.88).

Table 1–1 illustrates the benefits of a larger initial sum and higher interest rates on the compounding process. Having twice as much money in the beginning ($8,000) will reduce our schedule by at least three years. This is a vivid example of "time is money." The more money you have to begin your speculation, the sooner

TABLE 1–1   Approximate Time in Years to Reach $1 Million

Starting Principal	Length of Time at Compounded Rate of Return		
	12 percent	16 percent	24 percent
$ 4,000	48 years	36 years	24.5 years
8,000	42	32	21.5
12,000	38	29	20
16,000	36	27	18.5
20,000	34	26	17.5
24,000	32	24.7	17
28,000	31	23.5	16
32,000	30	23	15

your wealth expectations can be met and complete failure is less likely.

The 25 percent rate above is more than an example. It is a goal worth seeking, and anything less doesn't warrant the risk that the stock market presents. A good portion of this book is devoted to demonstrating that 25 percent is attainable and how this goal should influence your investing.

MAXIM 1–2   Plan for 25 percent average annual rate of return.

First we decide if we really want the risks and rewards of the stock market. Next we review our assets and isolate our speculative stake. Then we say good-bye to it, as it's in the army now and won't be available again until the war is over. We must now prepare ourselves to receive some good luck. As General MacArthur said: "Chance favors a prepared man."

SECURITIES MARKETS—A GAME OF CHANCE

Much has been written in recent years about the random character of stock market price formation. From Louis Bachelier's pioneering work *Theory of Speculation* written in 1900 to Burton Malkiel's *A Random Walk Down Wall Street* published in 1973, today's academics and their computers are grinding out evidence that tomorrow's stock prices are unpredictable. If price change is not perfectly random, it is close enough that the individual investor would be well advised to proceed on that assumption.

The evidence suggests to the theoretician that the markets are totally efficient, impossible to beat consistently, and consequently should be avoided. I believe the markets should be treated as any other game of chance and played only under favorable conditions. This philosophy might be stated formally as:

> *Theorem:* Securities markets behave as a game of pure chance and may be played successfully over extended periods only when there is positive mathematical expectation.
>
> *Corollary:* Whatever you do will be wrong—at least in the short run!

Since tomorrow's prices (or the next trade, for that matter!) are unpredictable, the chances are nearly 50 percent that those prices will be lower. Allow enough trades to take place or time to pass and the probability increases to well above 50 percent that the security will trade both above and below the current price. For that reason, whatever price is paid for a security will rarely be the low price for the near term, let alone for the year. Thus the prudent investor should adopt two principles:

1. You must accept emotionally the imperfection of the trading process. That means that you act on relative value and hold the security long enough for value to override random walk.
2. You should hedge against a "better" price by using the limit order to bargain unemotionally in your behalf. A probabilistic method of setting price is discussed in Chapter 5.

When I first came out of college and was introduced to the real work world, it stimulated my interest in early retirement to the point where I studied casino games and betting strategies. I was particularly attracted to published money management systems where bets were increased after losses in a systematic fashion until losses were recovered. I polished a revision of one of these for the roulette wheel and could even calculate my hourly rate of expected return from regular play. It seemed too good to be true, and my mathematician friends assured me that it was, because of negative mathematical expectation. In other words, the house percentage prevents a fair game.

Even though I had my bags packed for Las Vegas, I was cautious enough to try out the process on the computer. I ran a thousand trials, and it worked just fine. Another thousand verified my thinking. Still not convinced, I ran 10,000 trials at $1 per play, and the problem became clearly evident. At one point the system went $55,000 in debt; and worse, it required bets in excess of the $500 house limit.

Adjusting the system for the house limit and running additional cases proved futile, and my plans for early retirement via the casino route were abandoned. I have since used the system on a limited basis for entertainment, fully aware that eventual bankruptcy would result if the negative expectancy persisted. Now it is fairly well known that blackjack is the only casino game that can be played with positive expectation, and only at certain times after careful counting of the cards. A fresh deck will immediately remove any advantage. The stock market is similar in principle, as it offers a positive expectation if played correctly.

Members of the various securities and commodities exchanges trading with minimum fees have a very close approximation of a fair game. Taxes come after the profit and just reduce the expectation rather than turning it negative. The individual investor is not so fortunate, and the harder he tries to overcome the commission disadvantage by extra trading, the more aggravated the negative expectancy becomes. It sounds hopeless, but you can turn the odds in your favor, and you must do this if you are to survive a long-term investment horizon. Eventual ruin results otherwise!

The commissions can't be eliminated, but they can be combated by minimizing trades in favorable quantities and prices, discounted wherever possible. Use of the limit order can ensure that you get a price below what you normally pay or you don't buy. (Don't be stampeded by a broker crying that you'll miss the market.) What you'll get is a guaranteed good execution or none at all.

A sure way of paying the commissions is with dividends from the purchased security. The dividends are a significant positive factor for the buyer and just as negative for the short-seller. The dividends should be above average and secure. Historical return on the Dow Jones industrial stocks for the last 70 years consisted of 4 percent growth and 5 percent dividend. The argument that nondividend companies grow faster than their higher-yielding brothers is not borne out in statistical studies for a one-year holding period.

Taxes in general will reduce the positive expectation, but the current capital gains law can be used to turn taxes *positive!* For example, if you are in the highest tax bracket and have a net long-term gain in one year and a net short-term loss in the next year for an equal amount, the tax on the first year would be 20 percent of the gain. The tax bill in the second year would be reduced by an amount equivalent to 50 percent of the prior year's gain. Suppose you have a gain of $1,000. The tax is $200 if held to long term (see "Taxes," in Chapter 6). The following year you lose $1,000 short term. Your tax bill is reduced by $500. You are actually $300 ahead on taxes. This advantage holds regardless of your tax bracket. Losses must be taken short term and ordinary income turned into capital gains whenever possible.

Three other factors must be considered. Inflation is a negative, both in reduction of the buying power of your return and in the tendency of money to flow out of the stock market and into fixed-income securities or hard assets during inflationary times. Time and margin are amplifiers, enhancing either the positive or negative effect set in motion by the investor.

If you accept the discussion thus far, then it should be obvious that most of the exotic trading strategies offer negative expectation. Commodities are no better than a roulette wheel with taxes and commissions serving as zero and double zero. Options are even worse because of the leveraged commissions. Short selling is the poorest game in any market, as you are at cross-purposes with both inflation and dividends in addition to the loss of earning power on your money deposited to margin.

Most investors disregard the negative factors in favor of their ability to spot undervalued opportunities or developing "stories." The hard evidence is that the most brilliant investors are less than 60 percent correct in their selections. Normal commissions and sloppy tax planning will take care of that advantage.

The intelligent investor will use the dividend to neutralize both commissions and inflation. Long-term gains and short-term losses will add to a positive expectancy. Once the odds are in your favor, then the judicious application of margin will amplify return significantly. Do this systematically and the laws of statistical probability will make the markets pay off regardless of your ability to recognize "bargains."

Investing in quality stocks with good yields held long term is the only consistent winning strategy, as any long-term survivor of the markets will be happy to tell you.

MAXIM 1–3   The stock market is a game of chance that should be played only when the mathematical expectation is positive.

PRICE POTENTIAL PARADOX

In the preceding section we argued the case for daily price change having the appearance of random motion, and therefore we concluded that we should treat the stock market as a game of chance. This rules out trading, as the commissions create a negative expectancy that can't be overcome. So let's now consider long-term holding of stock and an apparent advantage that this allows.

Historical evidence shows a small upward bias in stock prices, averaging 4 percent annually over the past 65 years. Four percent is not enough to warrant a "buy and hold" strategy, and in trading once per year, commissions alone would offset the 4 percent. I don't believe the market to be strongly efficient, but I do believe that day-to-day price changes are random. For purposes of this argument I would assume the market to be a fair game, with neither an upward or downward bias.

The basis for this discussion is my conclusion that the stock market has a mathematical paradox that allows the knowledgeable investor a chance to realize a significant positive mathematical expectation from a fair game under random movement. To the best of my knowledge this has never been proposed before.

I'll first state the theory and then attempt to demonstrate the proof both by logic and through empirical evidence: If you seek a stock with enough volatility and give the investment enough time to develop, it has the potential to become worthless (price of zero) or to become priced in multiples of the original price. The most you can lose is 100 percent, but there is no limit on the upside: An appreciation of 1,000 percent is entirely possible. Putting the same dollar amount into two different stocks, where one appreciates 1,000 percent while the other loses 100 percent, sees the gain of 10 units in the first stock more than offsetting the loss of 1 unit on the second.

Seeking this much volatility is not practical, and the number of 100 percent losses would probably wipe out the occasional gain, similar to betting on a long shot on a roulette wheel. However, if we look for quality stocks that have 100 percent price appreciation

TABLE 1–2 Exponential Net Price Displacement Percent of Two Equal but Opposing Investments for Different Volatility Levels

Potential Percentage		Net Percentage of Profit
Gain	Loss	
400%	80%	160 %
300	75	113
200	67	66
100	50	25
50	33	9
20	17	1.6
10	9	.5

potential and if they trade over a stable range of prices, then buying at the bottom yields 100 percent while buying at the top depreciates capital by 50 percent.

For example, a stock trading between 10 and 20 yields 100 percent when bought at 10 and sold at 20. Conversely, buying at 20 and selling at 10 loses 50 percent. A dollar invested at each price would result in a $1 profit and a 50 cent loss. The net profit of 50 cents is 25 percent of the original $2 investment. Note in Table 1–2 how this net profit diminishes as we "expect" less and less price movement, until it becomes insignificant compared to taxes, commissions, and so forth.

The strategy that I have used successfully for over 24 years is to seek fundamentally sound stocks with enough volatility to allow a potential gain of 100 percent and to settle for less only under duress. This is not the risky game it first appears to be; there are plenty of A+ stocks with betas of 1.2 that will do very nicely (see Chapter 3). Two of my past 100 percent winners were Western Union and Eastman Kodak. I now hold Xerox with the same expectation. I am willing and expect occasionally to give up a 50 percent loss in order to allow enough time for the price changes to accrue in my favor. However, I clean out losers prior to the end of a six-month holding period in favor of short-term tax losses.

The logic behind this theory lies in the variation of the unit change in price as the stock takes on higher or lower prices. Stated a different way, the change expected is a fixed percentage of price rather than a fixed unit. For example, a $100 stock with an average change of 5 points (5 percent) would have an expected average change of 2.5 points (5 percent) when split 2 for 1 or would

FIGURE 1–3 Chart of Daily Stock Prices

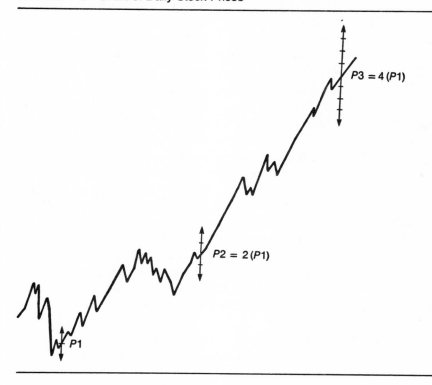

average 1 point in change for the same period of time when split 5 for 1.

This percentage change would at any point in time be equally likely up or down (random basis) and would vary with each stock, based on its individual volatility. The net result, up or down, over time would be the excess accrual of daily changes similar to coin flips where an excess of heads or tails eventually emerges. The difference here is that for the same accrual period a positive net would be larger than a negative one, because the most recent changes would be larger units in a rising stock and smaller unit changes as price declines.

First let's assume that the unit change does vary with price, and later we'll assume it doesn't. Figure 1–3 shows a rising stock initially priced at $P1$, which is half of the price reached at $P2$. $P1$ is one fourth the price of $P3$. When priced at $P1$ the average daily movement might have been one point up or down. The percentage change would be 1(100)/$P2$/2, which is 200/$P2$. When the stock advances to $P2$ the daily fluctuation averages two points up or down, or 2(100)/$P2$ percent (also 200/$P2$). At $P3$ a four-point daily variation would give 4(100)/2($P2$) percent (again 200/$P2$), so all three percentage changes are equal.

This may not be perfectly true of all stocks, as the trading increment of one eighth may distort the price change at the lower range and lower prices may attract more buyers, creating somewhat more volatility. But if we were to assume this relationship to be perfect, then a branch of mathematics called calculus can be used to show that prices will follow the curve $P = e$ to the kt power, where e is the constant 2.7183 . . . familiar to scientists, k is the stock's individual volatility constant, and t is time. The curve and its reflection are shown in Figure 1–4.

If a stock is at Price A, then it has equal likelihood to expand to Price C or contract to Price B. Going from A to C is a double (100 percent gain), while A to B is a 50 percent loss. If two stocks were at Point A and one went to C while the other went to B, equal dollar amounts in each would result in a 25 percent net gain for the investor.

Now let's reverse the argument and assume that price change is a consistent unit change regardless of price. That would mean that stock splits would raise the volatility of the stock. A $100 stock that varies by two points each day, if split 10 for 1, will still vary two points, or 20 percent per day. This definitely is untrue. The actual progress is probably neither a straight line nor exponential. The point is, if the line bends at all, then the long-term investor has an advantage.

The curve in Figure 1–4 assumes that k is the same constant for all price levels for a specific stock. The proof would require a large computer and a significant database, but it seems intuitive that the unit change would contract as P approaches the limit of zero for price and would expand as P increases. One hint that this is true is *Value Line Investment Survey* data plotted on a logarithmic (exponential) scale. This gives the price charts a linear (nonexponential) appearance.

If you look at exceptional market performance, the biggest gainers during the year are balanced by the largest losers on the exponential scale of Table 1–2. There are as many 75 percent losses as 300 percent gains. With my own personal record the same balance exists, including my largest loss of 88 percent com-

FIGURE 1–4 Potential Price Change as a Function of Time and Volatility

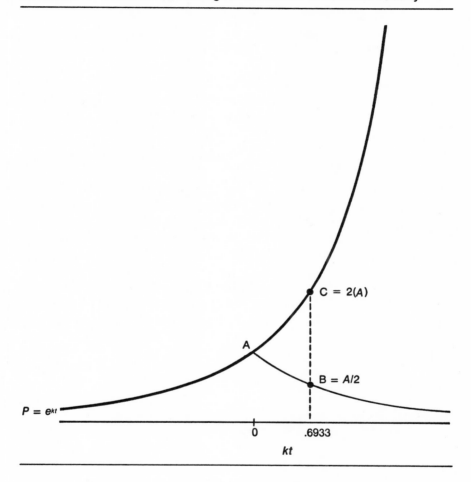

pared to my largest gain of 421 percent. My average gain is 115 percent and my average loss is 27 percent, resulting in an average annual net return of 26 percent. The average holding period for a winner was 490 days, while losers were held 232 days on average. The truncated holding period for losers, brought about for tax consideration, reduced the loss percentage proportionally.

If this theory is correct, then the desirable strategy is to play for large price appreciation potential in order to maximize net results. The old saw "You won't go broke taking a profit" is wrong if you are consistently satisfied with 20–30 percent gains. Still you must guard against issues being too speculative, as that might reduce the ratio of winners to losers. If your winning percentage falls far enough below 50 percent, then the positive net return will disappear. You also must take special care to allow enough time for winners to develop (at least to long term for tax purposes).

MAXIM 1–4 When selecting stocks, seek enough volatility and time for potential gains of 100 percent.

Acceptance of this strategy automatically eliminates certain investment vehicles. Short selling is in direct opposition to this theory. Options don't allow for enough price change (10 percent up is equivalent to 9 percent down) and have time limits that reduce net accruals. Stock index futures are the same. Commodity trading appears to be an area where application of this theory would be appropriate. *Certainly you must give up any thought of being satisfied with small-percentage winners.* The winning strategy is to buy fundamentally sound stocks and hold for a minimum of one year unless the stock is obviously a loser, in which case the sale must occur prior to the end of the short-term holding period for tax purposes.

PERFORMANCE POTENTIAL

Warren Buffett is a disciple of Benjamin Graham, who in turn was considered the father of security analysis. Graham was very successful as an investor, and Buffett has been even more so. Buffet managed an investing partnership from 1956 to 1969, and each dollar placed there at inception was worth $30 at the time he dissolved the fund. That's a rate of nearly 30 percent compounded annually.

Warren Buffett has set the standard that every investor should aspire toward. More-dazzling performers have come and gone, absorbing a maximum of media attention before they disappeared from the financial scene completely, but Buffett continues his performance with Berkshire-Hathaway at 22.1 percent compounded annually. Conservative, disciplined investing that ignores market action and noise and concentrates on out-of-fashion value at half-price has served him well.

John Templeton has applied similar methods, with his fund growing at approximately 16 percent per year over a 20-year period. Fund managers are at somewhat of a disadvantage, as they must overdiversify and report regularly to shareholders, which in turn feeds performance pressure back into the management process.

So what good is citing a couple of exceptions and aiming for their level of performance by the average investor? First, if you aren't prepared to seek exceptional performance, then the stock market is no place to be. An average performance, exemplified by return on the Dow Jones stocks for the past 70 years consisted of 4 percent growth and 5 percent dividend yield. You can guarantee more right now by buying long-term bonds and forgetting about the trials of the markets. Second, more people reach 20 percent return from the markets than you would think. Often it's a matter of self-protection to keep the results secret, but we have all heard the stories that surface from the obituaries. It's a little late then to ask how they did it. The fact that they have kept their success to themselves is a reflection of the discipline that you must have in order to excel.

Theoretically there is no limit to potential return from the markets. Most stocks trade over a 2 + percent range each day. If you could predict and play the daily ranges, the compounded annual rate would be 1,403 percent. Playing the intraday swings would send the rate off toward infinity. Before you get too excited, remember that you must have perfect foresight and somehow avoid the commissions, which will run more than 2 percent for a round-trip trade.

A buy-and-hold strategy will return 15–20 percent over an extended period for only a handful of stocks.

Had our foresight been as good as our hindsight and put us into Xerox at 11 in 1962, by 1972 we would have received a total return of 31.4 percent per year. Had we continued holding until 1982, then the total return would only be 22 percent for the 20-year period, with the dividend producing almost half of that. It still is an exceptional buy, but sale in 1972 and purchase of virtually any other stock would have been a better strategy. There always is some point when the buy-and-hold strategy should end.

We need to seek the middle ground: stocks held long enough to diminish the impact of commissions and to allow value to be recognized, but not so long as to enter a period of stagnant or negative growth. The consensus of people that have used this strategy successfully is one–three years. If the value you see is real, then it will be recognized or the company should have solved any problems depressing share prices in that time.

The goal to be sought is 25 percent annual return. The fact that only a small percentage of investors reach that level shouldn't discourage you. It should be encouraging that their success was not accidental and does not require superior intelligence, inside information, massive databases, or staff.

The same success is attainable by the average investor who is willing to watch his commissions and taxes, seek above-average dividends, be patient in the positioning process, and in general discipline himself to take the most probable course of action when required.

Figure 1–5 shows my year-end portfolio value since 1966 plotted against a growth curve of 35 percent. The 35 percent is composed of 25 percent annual return on all stock bought (after commissions) and 10 percent added value from application of margin. Note that there is a fairly consistent pattern, with the exception of 1973 and 1974. Mine is a readily attainable record by anyone disciplined enough to use the principles that are to be described in this book.

FAILURE AND CONTINGENCY

Jesse Livermore, the great speculator of the first three decades of this century, said that the factor contributing most to his success was his willingness to accept a loss. This from a man who was bankrupt four times and bounced back to millionaire status each time. Henry Ford was asked once what he would do if he were to lose his entire fortune. Ford thought for a second and then replied that he would have it all back within a year.

He may have been thinking of Billy Durant, a contemporary of his, when he said that. William Crapo Durant, founder of General Motors, was ousted by bankers in the tight money conditions of 1910. He came back with Chevrolet and regained control of GM in 1915 but was voted out in 1920 after running his personal debt to $20 million. He then took a fortune out of Wall Street in the 1924–29 market but was eventually wiped out in 1930. After more ups and downs, he died broke in 1947. Durant once said,

FIGURE 1–5 Author's Compounded Growth of 35 Percent Annually with Actuals

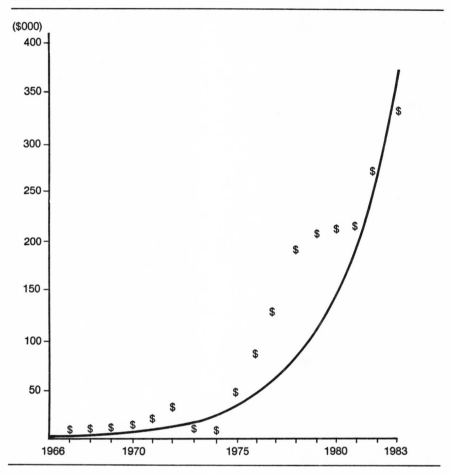

"Money is only loaned to a man: he comes into the world with nothing and leaves with nothing!"[2]

Anyone dealing with investments as volatile as the securities markets must be prepared for the certain losses, sometimes occurring in bankruptcy proportions. Livermore was the boldest of

---

[2]Dana L. Thomas, *The Plungers and the Peacocks* (New York, NY: Putnam Publishing, 1967).

FIGURE 1–6   Fifteen-Year Personal Trading Record (100 trades)

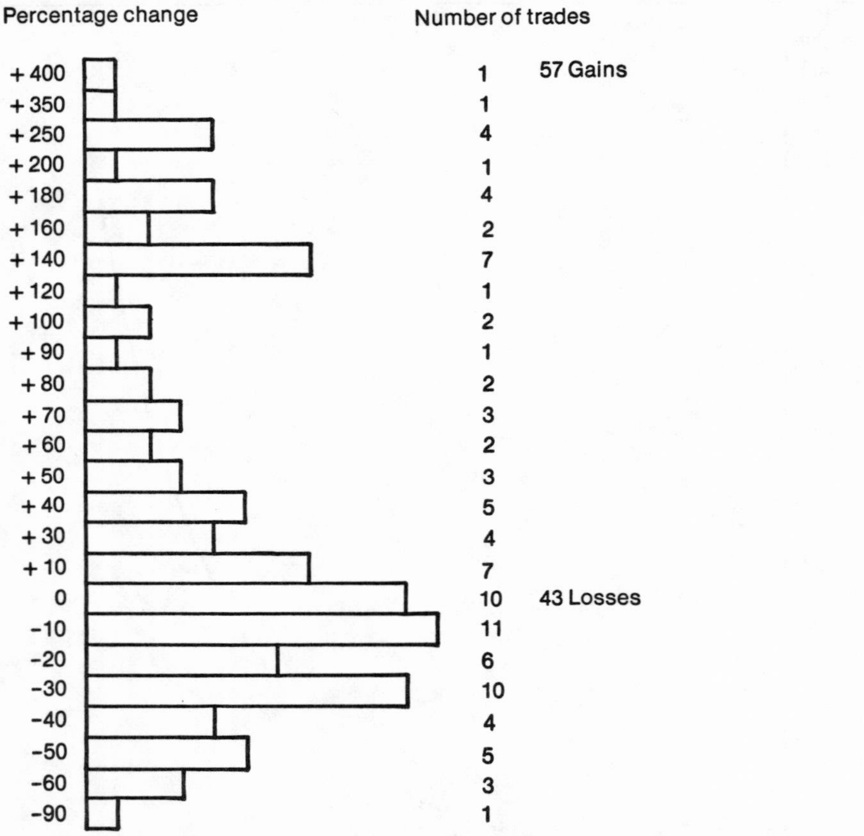

Percentage change   Number of trades

Percentage change	Number of trades	
+400	1	57 Gains
+350	1	
+250	4	
+200	1	
+180	4	
+160	2	
+140	7	
+120	1	
+100	2	
+90	1	
+80	2	
+70	3	
+60	2	
+50	3	
+40	5	
+30	4	
+10	7	
0	10	43 Losses
-10	11	
-20	6	
-30	10	
-40	4	
-50	5	
-60	3	
-90	1	

traders, and roller-coaster results were inevitable. The intelligent
investor will moderate his expectations in order to stay in the game
but still must be prepared for the large percentage loss. I expect
every fourth trade on average to be a loss of 30 percent or worse.
I feel that I must accept these in order to have enough volatility
and time for developing the one fourth of my trades that work
out to gains of 100 percent or more. The remaining 50 percent
contribute very little to either capital loss or gain (see Figure 1–6).
I'm looking for the one in four that is spectacular, accepting the
one in four that is significant loss and trying to squeeze dividends
out of the remainder.

I accept the loss by not letting it progress to long-term capital gains status. I sell for the tax advantage and the statistical edge this promotes. My contingency plan is to reposition in the stock if it continues to analyze positively. This requires objectively re-evaluating prospects and making a fresh set of decisions. Some of my most spectacular gains were significant losses earlier. I had short-term losses first, followed by long-term gains. More on this in Chapter 6.

Before entering any investment, a careful written analysis should be made, recording current conditions and stating reasons both for and against the decision. This document should also allow for expected development and serve to review the process periodically. If the schedule is not being met or the basic conditions change, then the contingency plan should be enacted. That could entail suspension of the positioning process or complete liquidation.

Liquidation would be warranted if fundamental changes (surprises) have occurred that would have kept you from considering the stock originally. As long as the fundamentals are still in place and the economic environment is favorable, you continue positioning or holding until the tax law enters the decision process, thereby taking it out of your hands.

The normal reaction to bad news is to sell, and most of the time this is a mistake. By the time you get the message, the insiders have already reacted, depressing the market. If the bad news is of a temporary nature or the effect on earnings is uncertain, then it may represent opportunity. However, if it is a significant development, such as a Chapter 11 declaration, then damage control is in order. That usually means an immediate sale to put the loss on the tax record and then some time to study the extent of the damage. Thirty days are required before reentering the stock to satisfy the short-term capital loss provision. If it's long term, it doesn't matter. After 30 days and with a clearer perspective, you may want to repurchase approximately half of your former holdings. The idea is to moderate some of the damage by taking advantage of the volatility created by the oversold condition of the stock. Recognize, however, that you will probably be faced with a short-term gain or an extremely long holding period while the company reorganizes. This also assumes that the asset value (book value) of the shares is higher than market price and attractive to possible takeover.

If the portfolio has been diversified, with a systematic positioning (see Chapter 5), then any failure should prove to be no more than a temporary setback for the portfolio. Weak markets are much more significant and must be waited out.

Regardless of the depressant, be prepared to undertake a particular course of action when it develops. Write out your intent beforehand, when the emotions are not part of the problem, and then let the mechanics take over when the crisis occurs. In the stock market, a crisis is as close to a sure thing as possible!

When a loss is finally established and you can be objective, conduct a postanalysis, reviewing your actions as good or bad under the information set that was available as each purchase was made. Such an analysis is not so important for successes, as you learn much more from the failures than from success. Remember the old saw "Prosperity is a good teacher, but adversity is better!"

MAXIM 1–5   Accept your losses and learn from them.

THE PLANNING WORKSHEET

A written plan for each stock purchase will provide incentive for an objective analysis and then serve as reference for periodic review as long as you hold the stock. Benjamin Franklin was known to make decisions by listing the reasons for the decision in one column and the reasons against in an adjacent column. He then proceeded to match and eliminate those in opposite columns of equal significance. When he finished, the remaining arguments were usually indicative of what he should do.

One of the most difficult things in the decision process is to decide which factors are important and which are trivial. This ability usually separates the successful from those less so. In selecting stocks the principal consideration should be the relative impact of the issue on the company's earnings per share. Since there is a market at the current price, both buyer and seller see reasons for their decision. If you are to outwit the other side of the trade, then you must find the most important factor confronting the company and analyze its resolution. By using Franklin's method, that issue will often emerge when the trivial items are scratched from the list. You can then focus on the future resolution of the central issue.

Figure 1–7 is an example of a worksheet that might be used by the individual investor. Modify it for your use and then pro-

FIGURE 1-7 Planning and Evaluation Worksheet

Planning Parameters: Stock_____ Date of analysis_____

Time frame: Months_____ Objective date_____ Commitment_____ Percent of portfolio_____

Current price____ Current value____ Book value____ Earnings objective____ Price____

Quick ratio _____Dividend yield _____12-month high _____12-month low _____

Economic Environment:

Interest rates _____ Direction _____ Comment _____

Inflation rate _____ Direction _____ Comment _____

Increase in GNP _____ Direction _____ Comment _____

Unemployment rate _____ Direction _____ Comment _____

Market Conditions:

Current DJIA _____12-month high _____12-month low _____

Model value_____ Percentage over/undervalued_____

Reasons for Purchase:	**Cautions:**
1. _____	1. _____
2. _____	2. _____
3. _____	3. _____
4. _____	4. _____
5. _____	5. _____

Purchase Record: **Sales Record:**

Date	Price	Amount paid	Date	Price	Amount received	Number of shares
_____	_____	_____	_____	_____	_____	_____
_____	_____	_____	_____	_____	_____	_____
_____	_____	_____	_____	_____	_____	_____
_____	_____	_____	_____	_____	_____	_____
_____	_____	_____	_____	_____	_____	_____
_____	_____	_____	_____	_____	_____	_____

duce copies to be readily available when stocks are under consideration.

The planning parameters force you to do a minimum amount of research on your candidate and to set down your objectives as to the total commitment to be made to the stock. Decide this now rather than after the buying program begins. Look forward to the objective date and estimate what expected annual earnings will be at that point. Use the value model (Chapter 4) to estimate price under those conditions. If the model is not twice the current price, look for another candidate. If current price is more than twice book value, look elsewhere. If the quick ratio is less than one, then avoid that stock; the prospects don't warrant the risk.

Chapter 3 is devoted to this analysis. Ideally the stock should be trading near the bottom of its 12-month range, have an average or better dividend yield, be selling below book value, and modeling at twice the current price. If you have other parameters that aid your analysis, then add them to your form and use them.

The Economic Environment section should make some statement about the condition of the economy. Though difficult to predict, if current conditions are at extremes, then it may influence your decision to buy or not buy. Difficult conditions are good opportunities, while "good times" may be the wrong time to commit to stocks.

The Market Conditions section is an attempt to get a handle on where overall stock prices fit into the normal business cycle. If the model shows the market to be 25 percent overvalued, then be cautious; 25 percent undervalued would be a significant opportunity. In most cases, you can ignore market conditions if the parameters are good for the individual stock.

The reasons for purchase should be clear, concise, and significant. Be objective. Likewise the cautions, or reasons not to buy, should be aired. The broker is good at filling the left-hand column, but you must dig through the investment services to complete the right side.

If the data has a positive (not optimistic) look, then you start your buying program as described in Chapter 5. Record the date, price, and amount. As each new purchase is contemplated, the entire form should be reviewed for accuracy. If major difficulties are encountered, then suspend the buying program and study the effect of the new information. The market probably knew this was coming and priced accordingly. If it destroys your original price objective, then sell your stock unless there is short-term profit in the shares being held. If so, let it run until it becomes a loss or the long-term date has been met.

Recently I completed a buying program on a computer communications company. The planning time frame carries into the end of 1985. At that point I expect earnings to be near $1 per share on an annual basis and the stock to be priced near 20. I bought shares on May 29, 1984, at 6.375; July 23, 1984, at 7.125; October 8, 1984, at 8.75; December 10, 1984, at 7.625; March 14, 1985, at 8.375 and April 4, 1985, at 7.75. I am fully positioned at an average price of 7.75 per share. If I sold now, there would be profit in all shares held, and they will all be long-term as of October 5, 1985. If there are no major developments, I hope to sell in the October 1985–January 1986 period and will compute any taxes for 1985 and 1986 before deciding in which year to record the sale.

My reasons for purchase were:

1. An established product.
2. An expanding market with little competition.
3. No debt, and significant cash.
4. The company principals have Xerox and Hewlett-Packard backgrounds and patronage.

My cautions were:

1. Future competition from major vendors as market expands.
2. Possible change in technology.
3. Little book value.
4. Possible premature expansion into competitive fields.

The company is selling its products, the earnings are expanding quarter to quarter, and neither my reasons nor my cautions have changed. Ultimately I will be proven right or wrong; regardless, I have done all I can at this time to ensure a good investment.

Having established my position, I no longer will be concerned with the price objective but now will focus on the time objective. In December 1985 I'll be much more concerned about the tax situation than whether the stock has reached 20 or 12 or 32. I'll take whatever the market gives me at that point unless there appears to be more to come. Much more is to be said about this later.

PERFORMANCE ANALYSIS

Just as it is good business to look forward, it is also important to look back. By analyzing our past performance we may be able to eliminate some mistakes in the future. You should look at both successes and failures—but especially failures! If you've done your planning worksheets, documenting your original impressions, you can now determine their validity. See if a common thread runs through most failed stocks. Possibly overoptimistic earnings forecasts or bad timing compounded with emotionally charged decisions. Or was it impatience? Perhaps a poor market chased you out of a good stock. Find your weakness and guard against it!

My father completed just a few years of elementary education but has run a successful business for 61 years. He may not be well educated, but he "knows whether he's making or losing a dollar!"

Do you know how you stand with your investments? We love to talk about the big killing that we made in the market, but what about the losses? How much did we have at risk, and how long did it take? A $5,000 profit may sound significant until we realize it was on a $50,000 investment and over five years coming to fruition.

Not one investor in a hundred knows his performance parameters. Even the notable successes, when asked how many of their purchases are ultimately successful, will only talk in generalities. They aren't being evasive—they just don't know! With the availability of the computer, how can you conduct business without knowing whether you're making or losing a dollar? Even before I had access to a personal computer, I kept each transaction invoice and recorded the vital information on a spreadsheet.

Table 1–3 is an example of five of my purchased stocks. The selections chosen were representative of my trading record. The purchase entries are the ticker symbol for the stock, the number of shares, date of purchase, price per share, gross amount (including commission), and the commission. The table also contains sales data on the same five stocks. Line 9 is the total dividend paid while I owned the stocks.

With this data you can conduct extensive analysis of each individual stock and prepare a running composite that will serve as a monitor during your learning process.

A number of interesting items will turn up with this simple set of data. For example, add lines 4 and 8 and compare with the total of line 9. You'll find that the dividends have more than paid

TABLE 1–3 Example of Investor's Stock Transaction Records and Data Analysis

			Ticker Symbol		
	MER	*GM*	*WU*	*EK*	*EK*
Number of shares	200	200	300	100	100
Purchase data					
1. Date of purchase	12/16/77	09/25/78	10/26/78	01/17/80	12/21/79
2. Price	$ 15.75	$ 63.50	$ 17.875	$ 49.25	$ 46.125
3. Amount	3,224.65	12,870.00	5,479.67	4,999.70	4,697.50
4. Commission	74.65	170.00	117.17	74.70	83.00
Sale data					
5. Date	04/19/78	07/11/79	09/15/80	02/02/81	02/02/81
6. Price	$ 15.00	$ 57.625	$ 28.125	$ 70.375	$ 70.375
7. Amount	2,931.86	11,360.40	8,338.48	6,952.47	6,952.47
8. Commission	63.36	158.00	89.36	82.80	82.70
9. Dividend	110.00	1,030.00	735.00	195.00	195.00
Analysis					
10. Days (5 − 1)	124	289	690	382	409
11. Gain (7 − 3)	$ −292.79	$ −1,509.60	$2,858.81	$1,952.77	$2,256.97
12. Gain plus dividend (11 + 9)	$ −182.79	$ −479.60	$3,593.81	$2,147.77	$2,451.97
13. Percentage [(12/3) × 100]	−5.66852 %	−3.72649 %	65.58442 %	42.95797 %	52.19733 %
14. Annualized [(13 × 365)/10]	−16.685562%	−4.706466%	34.693207%	41.046224%	46.581967%
15. Dollar days* (3 × 10)	399,856.6	3,719,430.0	3,780,972.3	1,909,885.4	1,920,459.5
16. Rate dollar days† (15 × 14)	−6,671,832.1	−17,505,371.9	131,174,054.7	78,393,583.9	89,458,781.1

*Total, line 15 = 11,730,603.8.
†Total, line 16 = 274,249,215.7.

NOTE: Annualized rate of return = $\dfrac{274,249,215.7}{11,730,603.8}$ = 23.37 percent.

for the commissions. Compare the total of lines 4 and 8 to the total of line 3, and you'll see that I paid slightly more than 3 percent commission rate. However, it becomes more meaningful when you analyze how hard each dollar has worked for each day employed—the Analysis section of Table 1–3.

Line 10 is the result of calendar time between line 5 and line 1. Thus Merrill Lynch (MER) was held 124 days. This information allows the remainder of the data to be annualized.

Line 11 is the difference between the purchase amount in line 3 and the sale amount in line 7. When line 9 is added to line 11 you get the total return (line 12) of the investment (see Chapter 3).

Dividing line 12 by line 3 and multiplying by 100 gives the percentage gain of the investment. Line 14 converts this to an annualized rate by multiplying by 365 and dividing by the number of days held (line 10).

Line 13 is the value used to construct Figure 1–6. Line 14 is more meaningful to you, as it allows you to spot the extremes and then conduct a more rigorous decision analysis from the planning worksheet.

Now we're down to lines 15 and 16. These categories by themselves are meaningless. The totals are what we seek, as we can then average the total effect of each dollar invested, for each day employed. Line 15 is dollar days. Line 16 is rate dollar days. When 16 is totaled algebraically (i.e., subtract the negatives) and divided by line 15, the result is the annualized rate of return. Try the calculation yourself. Remember to add the last three numbers in line 16 and subtract the first two.

For years I conducted this exercise by hand. It is now easily adapted to the computer and the many spreadsheet programs that exist. The data may be retained and "what if" games played to yield more information. What if I eliminate all income (utility or preferred) stocks and analyze just the speculative portion. What if I eliminate those that didn't pay dividends or those that did?

The use is much more than intellectual curiosity, as we shall demonstrate in Chapter 5 when we use this analysis to determine the optimal number of stocks to be held in your portfolio.

After you conduct an analysis of your own trading record and have the percentage gain or loss corresponding to line 13 in Table 1–3, compare the results to my record for 100 trades in Figure 1–6. Are the two records similar? If not, where is the difference and why? If they are similar, as I would expect (with any major difference resulting from length of time held), then go one step farther and plot your year-end portfolio value against mine of Figure 1–5. Just find on my chart the year that has value corresponding to the value of your starting year and plot forward from that point.

How does your plot look? If your record is similar to Figure 1–6, but not similar to 1–5, then the problem is money management. Chapter 6 should help. The problem reduces to one or more of these elements: time, commissions, dividends, taxes, or margin.

Plan and evaluate. Get acquainted with where your money has gone, and you may be able to prevent it from frequenting the wrong places.

CHAPTER 2

Wealth Principles

Money doesn't bring happiness, but it calms the nerves.
—*French Proverb*

Some of the best investment advice can be found in the biographies of the money masters of the past—not in what they say but in what they do. Often these entrepreneurs weren't fully aware of the factors contributing to their success, but it is fairly obvious that they shared a number of traits in common.

The principles they employed are just as sound today, even though we face somewhat different problems than they encountered. Taxes, for example, are significantly more worrisome today than they were for Bernard Baruch and Arthur Cutten, and both expressed doubts about repeating their successes under heavier tax burdens. Commissions have changed significantly since the first brokers gathered under the buttonwood tree in New York and agreed to charge the public .25 percent as commission. Today's commissions can run as high as 10 percent, depending on the investment vehicle, and for most investors this becomes an obstacle that is rarely negotiated properly.

Manipulation of markets in the past was common and was the modus operandi of such famous Wall Street personalities as Daniel Drew, Jay Gould, Jesse Livermore, and even Bernard Baruch. The markets are well regulated now, so that manipulation is very difficult, if not impossible. Still many of these market legends would do well today because of their use of fundamental principles. The four characteristics that seem to be shared by the very wealthy are work, sacrifice, leverage, and discipline.

WORK

From time immemorial, fathers have advised their sons that the secret of wealth is "work and save." This advice is not enough, but it is a good place to start. Work is a consistent theme in all self-made wealth; but most important, the work must be properly directed. Just working hard doesn't guarantee anything, as the poor will be quick to verify. Most work is directed to subsistence, with the fruits of that labor consumed. It is work that is in excess of earning your daily bread that starts the wealth process. For today's wealth seeker, that means a broad reading program, screening investment candidates, and a systematic evaluation process.

In my 25 years of stock market interest, I have read nearly 1,500 books on the subject. I currently read or reread over 75 per year, even though there is rarely anything new discussed. I read the bad along with the good—if nothing else, just to know what to avoid. More and more of my reading is directed toward biographical material to further verify and focus my own principles. Reading helps to maintain my perspective, especially the classical texts on the subject (see Appendix C, "Recommended Reading List"). I try to instill this principle in my seminar students but with very little success. Most people are looking for shortcuts, and most people fail at investments.

Often I'm asked where I find my companies, and the answer is relatively obvious. I try to concentrate on stocks in my fields of interest, located nearby, or a product line so simple that I can understand and anticipate their business. I construct a "shopping list" that I use over and over as companies go through their cycles. This "rifle" approach is not an original idea; Andrew Carnegie employed it to the extreme, often knowing more about a company's operation than did the principal operating officers. Warren Buffett does exactly the same thing today, with immense success.

You don't have to be an insider to have enough understanding of a company to be able to invest wisely. There is plenty of public information that goes largely untouched by the average investor. This kind of study will probably help your appraisal of value, but it definitely provides an emotional foundation for evaluating new information and the market's reaction to its release. Nothing panics an investor more than not understanding a new development.

For the financially successful the work ethic was instilled early, under abject poverty for most of those to become extremely wealthy. The incentive was underlined by their poverty, unlike those born to wealth. The ability to build more wealth from a base of wealth is well known (it takes money to make money), but most inherited wealth has a way of disappearing, or stabilizing, from a lack of incentive to extend it. There are exceptions, most notably the superwealthy Howard Hughes and John Paul Getty; but considering the potential for "money begetting money," look at the extremely wealthy of the past and their struggle to retain the purchasing power of their inherited wealth. The farsighted Andrew Carnegie and John D. Rockefeller distributed much of their wealth through foundations for the good of mankind.

Carnegie was approached by a reporter who said, "Mr. Carnegie, don't you think you should distribute your wealth to the less fortunate of the world?" Andrew looked at him for a moment and then instructed his secretary: "Get me the latest figures on my wealth and the world's population." When the figures were provided, Carnegie pulled the stump of a pencil out of his pocket, did some arithmetic on the back of an envelope, and then told his secretary: "Give this man 2 cents—that's his share of my fortune!" Carnegie knew what he was going to do with his money, and it's to our everlasting benefit that he did.

There is a positive correlation between effort and results. Sometimes a very little extra effort provides the answer that shapes your decision. For instance, to verify rumors about a company, I have called the investor relations or public information office, confronting them with the question. Their carefully rehearsed answers have sometimes verified the information that I was seeking.

Recently I was interested in a new public offering and sought more information than was in the prospectus. There is an operations report (10-K) that is available, but I wanted the "feel" of the company. So I took a trip into their area, walked into my company, announced that I am a shareholder, and asked to see the investor relations manager. This resulted in an impromptu tour with one of the founding engineers, and I came away with a solid description of their problems and how they are dealing with them. Don't forget to check the reception area and the garbage bins, as any good detective would, to find out whom they deal with and the volume of business conducted.

SACRIFICE

You can't have your wealth and consume it too! Ben Franklin of the "penny saved is a penny earned" school also said, "The way to wealth, if you desire it, is as plain as the way to market. It depends chiefly on two words, industry and frugality; that is, waste neither time nor money, but make the best use of both."[1]

Daniel Drew, always ready with a homily, said, "Better a chicken tomorrow than an egg today!"

Franklin would have understood John D. Rockefeller, who as a boy hoed potatoes dawn to dusk for a neighbor for 37 cents per day. He accumulated $50, which he then loaned back to the same neighbor at 7 percent interest, marveling that the annual interest was worth 10 days' work: "It was better to let the money be my slave, than to be the slave of money." At 16 he worked in Cleveland as a bookkeeper, starting at $15 per month and in three years advancing to $50 per month. He saved $800 during that time. With that kind of early training, it is really not difficult to understand his careful rationing of dimes to the general public in later years?

Andrew Carnegie was raised in Scotland by a mother who had parted company with the Calvinistic Presbyterian Church but taught Andrew from her own personal catechism. On the first day of school, the children were asked to recite their favorite proverb, to which Andrew responded, "Take care of the pence, and the pounds will take care of themselves."

The schoolmaster frowned and the children tittered, but Carnegie was well informed. As a 14-year-old in the United States, he worked at grueling labor in a bobbin factory, and every cent went to the family's survival. Later, as a telegraph operator, his salary went to the purchase of their first home. Would anyone raised under these circumstances spend money frivolously?

Savings alone will not create real wealth, but you have to have some money to prime the pump.

This money must not be needed for survival and must be thought of as being available until your objectives are met. I can agonize over phone bills or car repairs but be totally calm over daily fluctuation by thousands of dollars of my portfolio. One is "real" dollars, the other is my "play" money. If you look around you for the truly wealthy, it's likely to be the person living in

---

[1]Benjamin Franklin, *Poor Richard's Almanack* (New York: David McKay, 1961).

modest circumstances, driving a beat-up car (or walking), rather than those living in luxurious surroundings. In *Rogues to Riches*, Murray Bloom chronicles three individuals that turned up in the obituaries with multimillion dollar estates created in the market while living under conditions near poverty. In all cases, they considered their stock fund untouchable. This was exemplified by one as he was checked into the hospital, saying, "I don't know how I'm going to pay for this!"

LEVERAGE

Archimedes said, "Give me a place to stand and I'll move the earth." He was extolling the capabilities of physical leverage, but financiers have adopted his principle to the world of finance—in short, borrowed money.

Historically there were only three ways to wealth! Steal, inherit, or borrow. Today we also have the lottery. But before you win a million-dollar lottery, you're more likely to be struck by lightning—10 times!

Marriage can be a form of inheritance, but a Scottish proverb warns that marrying money is more expensive than borrowing. Kin Hubbard said, "Nobody works as hard for money as the man that marrys it."

So what it boils down to is borrowing—and our impoverished millionaires-to-be never hesitated to borrow money for their ventures, even though in later life they often sat on their pile and advised others to "never borrow."

Andrew Carnegie conducted an amazing parlay that raised his income from less than $1,000 per year to over $42,000 in seven years.

The Carnegies came to the United States from Scotland in 1848, when Andrew was 13. They had to borrow £20 (about $100) for passage. In America, Andrew was pressed into work at $1.20 per week to help support the family, and his mother saved half-dollars from his pay to repay their loan. By age 20 Andrew was working for the Pennsylvania Railroad at $30 per month, and the Carnegies were buying a house for $550 on a two-year repayment schedule.

One day Carnegie's employer asked if he would like 10 shares of Adams Express stock that a friend wanted to sell for $60 per share. Without hesitation, Andrew said yes and then worked out this arrangement:

1. He asked his boss to give him six monthly installments to pay the $600.
2. He then went to a moneylender and at a high rate of interest borrowed the first installment.
3. His mother borrowed the remainder from her brother in the form of a second mortgage on their house.
4. Andrew paid the balances from his salary and dividends on the stock.

Three years later he managed a 12.5 percent interest in the Woodruff Sleeping Car Company and was given an installment payment schedule in return for promotion of the venture. He went to a bank, apparently used Adams Express as collateral, and borrowed the first payment of $217.50. After that, dividends on his two companies covered the installment payments.

Three years after this, dividends from his first two investments were used to buy into Columbia Oil, and by age 28 his income had risen to $42,260.67 (tax return), with only $2,400 as salary.

Compared to the Rothschilds, Carnegie was a piker. We are told the story of how the Rothschilds' information system (carrier pigeons?) relayed to them the news of Napoleon's defeat at Waterloo. In London, Nathan Rochschild personally sold into the London market and then had his agents buy the depressed stocks before the course of the battle was known by the public.

Good story, but a better one tells where his purchasing power came from. The elder Rothschild (Mayer Amschel) was a rare-coin dealer in Frankfurt who worked his way into the court of Duke William of Hesse. When the Napoleonic wars broke out, Mayer (with great foresight) placed his son Nathan in London and conducted financial transactions for the Duke. William was extremely wealthy from having supplied a steady stream of Hessians for service to England in the American Revolution.

As Napoleon overran Germany, the Duke avoided confiscation by empowering the Rothschilds to buy bonds in the London markets. By the time Nathan received the funds, quotations had dropped, and Nathan decided to wait and put the money to use for his own purposes. Although the Duke pressed for the certificates, the blockade of the continent by Napoleon was used as an excuse for nondelivery. The money was used for three years by the Rothschilds in the very lucrative money markets created by the war. At war's end, the bonds were purchased and sent to the Duke, and the Rothschilds were established.

Other people's money (OPM) is the theme that is drummed into real estate investors. We recognize that a business or real estate investment requires borrowed funds, but we are hesitant to borrow for other forms of investment. We must recognize the securities markets as a business and fund our selections accordingly. Failure is possible, as it is in a small business or in a house that we can't resell; but I would suggest that the risk, if properly managed, is no worse in the stock market than in any other form of investment.

DISCIPLINE

The dictionary defines discipline as self-control. This is the keystone characteristic for success in any endeavor. I like to think of discipline as doing what you don't want to do. You must control your emotions and act boldly and objectively on the basis of the facts, when the occasion demands. Conversely you must exert patience when action is not warranted.

Reasonable plans for attaining financial security often involve up to 20 years without touching the principal and occasionally mean scraping up additional cash at the expense of reduced living standards. That kind of self-denial and dedication to goals requires the finest form of discipline.

Most investors are not disciplined, and most investors do the wrong thing. They buy after the markets have progressed steadily to new highs and sell when prices are driven toward new lows. Daniel Drew says that he tried to calculate what the common man was going to do and then do the opposite. Ed Beckley, while promoting real estate seminars, says: "If you want to be truly rich, watch what the poor people do—and then don't do it!"

In market panics, the truly disciplined come to the front. Henry Clews, market watcher at the turn of the century, said that in times of panic, old men leaning on canes hobble into the financial district like spiders leaving their webs before rain, conduct their buying, and then disappear again into their homes until the next opportunity arrives.

Discipline brings a J. P. Morgan into the markets in the Panics of 1884 and 1907. He not only benefits personally but lends stability to a market under pressure. Discipline is the factor that makes Andrew Carnegie refuse to sign the notes of his mentor Thomas Scott, after warning him about overextending his expansion just prior to the Panic of 1873. Carnegie said that it was the most difficult thing that he had ever had to do. That same discipline allowed Carnegie to continue building a million-dollar steel plant during that same depression, with money scarce but materials and labor bargain priced. The reduced expense created an imminently profitable plant and a significant advantage on his competition.

It's hard to read the biographies of the great men without getting a feel for their ethics, or lack thereof. Jacob Little, Commodore Vanderbilt, Daniel Drew, Jay Gould, Jim Fisk, Jim Keene, and Collis Huntington would battle each other over railroads without mercy, in and out of court, bribing councilmen and legislators, using deceptive stock manipulation, and then at the next moment would align themselves with one that they had just beaten against one that had been their "pard." It was all considered to be "doing business."

Right or wrong ethically, what they did was without emotion and with complete self-control. They acted boldly when the occasion demanded and could wait patiently when that was the best course of action. The disciplined investor is the successful investor.

CHAPTER 3

Investment Tools

Nothing can have value without being an object of utility.
—*Karl Marx*

Some digression is now in order to ensure that everyone understands the techniques of Chapters 4 and 5. The nature of the discussion is tutorial and referential and can be bypassed by the student of fundamental analysis and modern portfolio theory. I propose to keep the discussion simple and nonrigorous, and I only intend to discuss those elements that are consistently of use to me in my investment practice. I'll try to describe each as I might a shovel or a wrench and defer to later chapters the discussion of how they apply to my strategy.

EARNINGS PER SHARE

Every public company is required to prepare an annual statement of income. That statement reports net sales, with attendant cost of sales and operating expenses. The sales, less expenses, represent pretax profits for the year. After computing and subtracting taxes, interest on bonds, and dividends paid to preferred stock owners, the balance (if any) is recorded as annual earnings.

Since the total dollar amount of earnings is difficult for the average investor to relate to, a comparison is made of earnings to the total shares of common stock outstanding. This figure is annual earnings per share and is an item eagerly awaited by the investment community. It commands more interest and is more instrumental in determining market price of the stock than is other element of information available on a company.

Share prices move in unison with the variation in earnings. If earnings increase, the stock price increases. If they fall, the share price falls. It is of utmost importance to anticipate the future course of earnings. If the earnings are relatively stable and predictable, then the market price will also be predictable and there is very little chance for the individual to find a bargain. It is in the unstable periods that the astute investor may find the bargains. Often this entails buying the stock after the company has reported lower earnings or a loss for the most recent reporting period. Interim reports showing recent results are issued every three months.

A reversal in earnings often turns the market pessimistic on company prospects, and shares may sell below value. If the condition impacting earnings is irreversible, then the bargain hunter may suffer significant loss of capital. However, if the poor earnings picture appears to be temporary, then an appraisal of reported earnings can serve as the basis of true or intrinsic value of the stock. An average of two or three recent years' reported earnings should be a reasonable goal as soon as the problem is corrected. Still, two questions must be answered:

1. Will the company be restored to profitability?
2. How long will it take?

A related item that is closely followed by investors is the price-earnings ratio (P/E). This is determined from the current market price divided by annual earnings per share. This number varies widely from company to company, dependent on growth prospects and the interest level of the stock market. Often the investor arbitrarily assigns a number that he feels to be reasonable and then uses projected earnings to place an optimistic value on the stock. In Chapter 4 we'll try to improve the valuation process by substituting for the P/E ratio.

A more meaningful ratio is the inverse of the P/E ratio, the E/P ratio. This is earnings yield and represents the profit return on the company if all shares were bought at the market price. Treating your stock purchase as if you were buying the entire company is the only way to evaluate stock price.

MAXIM 3–1 Buy each share of stock as if you were buying the entire company.

If you did purchase the company, then you could declare all profits as dividends to yourself or you could reinvest as much as desired toward development of the company. On that basis you would be interested in the yield that your investment produces, and the earnings yield would be indicative. In times of high interest rates, earnings yield would increase (P/E would fall) as other investments become more attractive. The process reverses as interest rates fall. Older companies are less attractive for the future, and therefore more current yield is expected (lower P/E). Dynamic new companies are more attractive, and thus investors are willing to take less current yield in deference to anticipated earnings growth in the future.

BOOK VALUE

In good times, annual earnings per share is the principal determinant of share price; however, when trouble is encountered, asset value of the company comes center stage. If the company is taking losses, then the investor has to think in terms of liquidation, and net assets represent the possible payback to the common shareholders. Often the assets are overstated, and the debt burden usually increases as a company struggles to stay solvent. Book value carries no guarantee, but it does often signal the floor value under share prices.

A stock bought at book value may proceed to 50 percent of book and thereby create a significant loss. Worse is the stock bought at three or four times book value that encounters an earnings setback that may also send prices to 50 percent of book.

As part of the required annual reporting, each public company produces a report called the balance sheet. This report balances company assets on one side against liabilities and stockholders' equity on the other side.

Basically, book value is the shareholder's equity or the difference between assets and liabilities after a couple of adjustments. The adjustments are a reduction in the equity by any intangibles reported and any preferred stock at par value. This adjusted equity is divided by the number of common shares outstanding and is called net book value per share of common stock. Most investment services list this or equity per share in their publications.

A ratio carefully watched and often quoted as a measure of a company's growth prospects is the return on equity. This is basically the annual earnings per share for the current year divided by last year's net book value per share. Return on equity varies widely by industry and probably is best used for comparison across years in the same company. It doesn't figure into any of the processes to be discussed later in this book and is only identified here as a convenience for those that do make use of this value.

CASH FLOW

Inspection of the annual report is primarily a defensive measure undertaken to see if a bargain-priced stock to which you're attracted has termites in the financial foundation. Book value is a good reference point. The next concern is the possible erosion of the book value by a squeeze on working capital. This expansion or contraction of working capital is termed cash flow.

The net working capital of a company is the current assets (cash, inventory, accounts receivable, and marketable securities) less the current liabilities (taxes, accrued expenses, notes, and accounts payable). This is the money available from profits and depreciation after current obligations are met. Occasionally a company will have as much working capital as the total market value of the common stock. That means that you could buy the company for the cash alone and receive all property, buildings, etc., as a bonus. Benjamin Graham describes the search for these companies in *The Intelligent Investor*. Normally we are only concerned that a company have enough cash to meet the immediate demands and that this cash is not shrinking.

A good way of measuring this relationship of ready cash to debt is the quick ratio. You compute it by subtracting inventory value from current assets and divide by current liabilities. The idea is that the inventory might not be readily marketable or properly valued, and the quick ratio determines if there is enough ready cash to meet obligations. A ratio of 1 or better is adequate and applies regardless of the type of product or service. I prefer the quick ratio to the more popular current ratio because of the exclusion of inventory and the more uniform result across industry lines. The intent is not to find strong companies but rather to spot the truly troubled ones and avoid them. It is not an easy chore and is subject to the interpretation of the analyst. The guiding rule is that bargain-priced stocks have problems. The analysis becomes a matter of determining the extent of the problem and judging whether it is correctable.

TABLE 3–1 Sample Heights

Height	Absolute Deviation	Variance
77 inches	7.375	54.390625
68	1.625	2.640625
69	.625	.039625
67	2.625	6.890625
72	2.375	5.640625
68	1.625	2.640625
67	2.625	6.890625
69	.625	.390625
557 ÷ 8 = 69.625		79.524000 ÷ 7 = 11.360571

STATISTICAL MEASURES

In the study of mathematical statistics, the methods are ordered around two functions: Descriptive statistics is the science of measuring and classifying data collections. Inferential statistics deals with producing decision-making information from the measured data. Both subjects are taught in college-level introduction-to-statistics courses with arithmetic the only prerequisite.

The use of standard statistical tools has promoted research and created an expanding theory regarding the management of investments. This area of study is called modern portfolio theory, or MPT. Practical developments include a measure of volatility (beta) and diversification methods. For an excellent treatment of the topic, consult Robert Hagin's *Modern Portfolio Theory*.

For our purposes we'll just skim the subject, introducing enough statistics to show the origin of the applications in later chapters.

Descriptive Statistics

A significant tool of descriptive statistics is standard deviation. It is a measurement of variation in data. A relatively small deviation would imply fairly uniform data, while a relatively large number suggests variety or instability. In other words the standard deviation measures the dispersion, or "scatter," of data around the average value.

If we consider the sample heights of Table 3–1, the simple summing of the eight entries and division by eight gives a mean (average) value of 69.625 inches. This technique alone can be useful if we were to apply it to annual earnings of a company or

FIGURE 3–1 Frequency Distribution

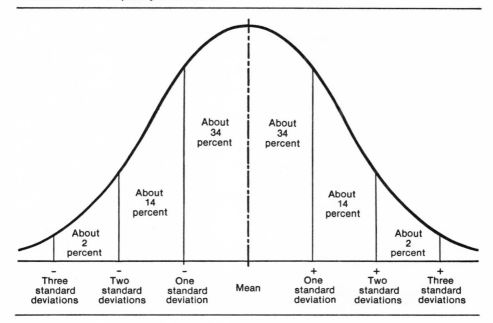

year-end stock prices or annual returns on your mutual fund. Knowing the average (mean) value is the first step, and determining the tendency of the data to be uniform or to vary widely is the next step. If we compare each individual in our eight-person sample to the average height of 69.625 inches, we can compute a deviation for each. The first height of 77 inches is 7.375 inches greater than the average. This is called the absolute deviation, and computing and summing for each of the eight values in our sample would give the average absolute deviation for the group.

However, this is rarely used as it is difficult to relate to. In the 19th century a Russian mathematician found that you could classify deviation of data from the mean value by use of a calculation called standard deviation (see Figure 3–1). The computation starts by multiplying each absolute deviation by itself: 7.375 times 7.375 equals 54.39065. This is termed the variance and is directly useful in some statistical processes.

When we sum the individual variances for our eight values and divide by the number of samples less one $(8 - 1)$, then we get a number that represents average variance. Division by seven rather than eight in our example is a refinement that statisticians have found to be more accurate in practical application.

Since we multiplied each deviation by itself (squared), to get our average in terms of deviation we reverse the process and take the square root (the number multiplied by itself that gives the variance). This is standard deviation. For our sample in Table 3–1 this becomes 3.3705446, and the following assumptions can be made about our example:

1. About 68 percent of our sample population will have a height within one standard deviation (3.3705446 inches) of the mean value of 69.625.
2. About 95 percent will have a height within two standard deviations (6.7410892 inches) of the mean height.

To the investor this is useful in a number of ways. Price variation can be measured in terms of standard deviation and then used to represent risk, as we shall do in the next section. Options players use it to determine inconsistencies in the market prices of puts and calls. A popular model used to calculate options values is the Black-Scholes method, which focuses on the standard deviation of the underlying stock price.

Descriptive statistics can be used for comparison: the risk (standard deviation) of one stock price to another; the mean return from one mutual fund compared to another.

The data can be compared, but very little can be concluded about future data points. Using inferential statistical methods, we will try to forecast future value.

Inferential Statistics

There are two basic types of forecasting. The first is time series, which assumes that time is the motivation for new value and that trends can be determined and extended as each new point in time is reached. There are a variety of methods, but the one most seen by investors is the moving average. This involves calculating the mean value of several data points, using that to represent the current point in time. As each new value in the data series is recorded, a new mean is calculated by including the new point in the averaging process and discarding the oldest. The calculation of this series of averages allows smoothing of the actual results and calculation of trend extension (forecast). Technical analysis

TABLE 3–2 Moving Average of Earnings

Year	Earnings	Three-Year Average	Double Moving Average
1975	$2.71		
1976	3.16		
1977	3.80	$3.22	
1978	4.18	3.71	
1979	3.07	3.68	$3.54
1980	4.51	3.92	3.77
1981	5.06	4.21	3.94
1982	5.77	5.11	4.41
1983	6.69	5.84	5.05
1984	7.33	6.60	5.85

uses the 200-day moving average for stock price trends. Securities analysts may use this technique to project earnings.

Table 3–2 is an example of how time series could be used to estimate earnings for the next year, where the earnings have been steadily growing. The prediction is:

$$Y = a + bX$$

where:

Y = Forecasted earnings.

X = Number of points (years) ahead for the prediction.

a = Two times the latest moving average, less the latest double moving average.

b = Two times the difference between the latest moving average and the latest double moving average, all divided by the number of points being averaged less one.

Using Table 3–2 data as an example:

$$a = (2 \times 6.60) - 5.85 = 7.35$$

$$b = \frac{2(6.60 - 5.85)}{3 - 1} = \frac{1.5}{2} = .75$$

$$X = 1 \text{ year ahead}$$

$$Y = 7.35 + (.75 \times 1) = \$8.10$$

So the estimated earnings for 1985 would be $8.10.

The choice of three years in the averaging process is arbitrary and would increase for larger sets of data. The larger the number of points being averaged, the smoother the resulting curve will be (more wiggles in the actual data will disappear). If you have a computer, the program is in Chapter 10.

The second method of forecasting is time independent and is categorized as causal. Inflation *causes* interest rates to change, for example. Time may or may not be a factor, but a relationship exists that shows dependence of one variable on another. A person's weight in great part depends on his or her height (as a generality, tall persons are heavier).

Using a technique known as regression analysis, we shall develop an estimating equation that will relate unknown variables to the known ones. Then we will extend the process slightly in a technique called correlational analysis. This determines the degree of the relationship.

Correlational analysis is useful in studying various market issues. For example, a panelist on a well-known investment show one night declared that given a choice of two stocks, one paying a dividend and one not, you should choose the nonyielding stock, as more growth could then be expected. This sent me scurrying to the computer with *Value Line Investment Survey* data, to do the following:

1. Compute the change in price of all stocks from January 1 to December 31.
2. Put this in percentage form for each stock.
3. Compute the amount yielded by each stock based on the January price.
4. Relate the percentage growth to percentage yield through correlation analysis.

The analysis showed no relationship at all between growth of price and dividend yield. The panelist may have been correct for longer periods of time; but I was only interested in my planned holding period of one year, and to me the opposite course (accepting the dividend) was the correct action.

Table 3–3 extends the height data of Table 3–1 to include weights of our sample population. The three extra columns are needed to derive a forecasting equation that will allow us to estimate a person's weight when given his or her height.

Let's digress for a second and qualify this data we're using. First of all, the points are real values given to me by eight male students in a seminar. Males were chosen to eliminate one variable (sex) in the forecasting equation. There are other determinants

TABLE 3–3 Sample Heights and Weights

Height (X)	Weight (Y)	Height × Height (X²)	Weight × Weight (Y²)	Height × Weight (X · Y)
77 inches	210 pounds	5,929	44,100	16,170
68	145	4,624	21,025	9,860
69	164	4,761	26,896	11,316
67	170	4,489	28,900	11,390
72	185	5,184	34,225	13,320
68	175	4,624	30,625	11,900
67	150	4,489	22,500	10,050
69	157	4,761	24,649	10,833
C1 = 557	C2 = 1,356	C3 = 38,861	C4 = 232,970	C5 = 94,839

of one's height (age, for example, and frame size), but height is probably the best single variable to estimate weight. The estimating equation probably won't be exact for 1 person in 10, but it should underestimate as many as it overestimates. Applied to stocks, determining whether price is over or under value would give a significant advantage.

Notice that each column of Table 3–3 has been totaled. These totals are needed to determine our forecasting equation. Also needed is the mean height and mean weight. The average height ($\overline{X}$) is 557/8, or 69.625 inches. The average weight ($\overline{Y}$) is 1356/8, or 169.5 pounds.

Using algebra, a straight line can be represented by the equation $Y = a + bX$. a and b are constants (set values for the line), while X and Y represent the varying elements of the equation. In our example, X represents height and Y is the corresponding weight. Figure 3–2 illustrates the set of men used for Table 3–3 as points, and the line defines the best representation of the entire population. If the relationship were perfect, then the points would all fall on top of the line.

This regression line can be used to forecast. Given a person's height and using Figure 3–3, we move to the right along the horizontal axis (base) of the graph until we reach the given height. We then move vertically until we intercept the regression line. At this point we move horizontally left until we reach the vertical axis (left boundary). The value at that point is representative of a man's weight for the given height. For example, John Doe stands 73 inches tall. Finding the vertical line marked as 73, we move upward until the diagonal line is reached. Moving left we reach the weight axis at 188 pounds.

Height and weight in our illustration could just as easily be inflation rate versus Treasury bill rates or dividend yield versus price growth percentage or a thousand other related variables.

The steepness (slope) of the diagonal line is measured as a ratio of weight change per unit of height change. As you can see from the graph, each inch of height is equivalent to over 5 pounds of weight. This ratio is called b in our forecasting equation and is computed from the totals of Table 3–3 by the following formula:

$$b = \frac{C5 - (N \cdot \overline{X} \cdot \overline{Y})}{C3 - (N \cdot \overline{X} \cdot \overline{X})}$$

Remember $\overline{X}$ is the average height (69.625 in our example) and $\overline{Y}$ is the average weight (169.5 pounds). N is the number of

FIGURE 3–2   Plotted Heights, Weights, and the Regression Line

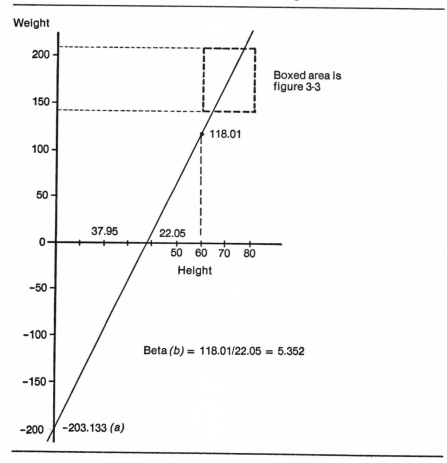

values (8) in the data set. Substituting our computed values in the equation for b and doing the arithmetic:

$$b = \frac{94{,}839 - (8 \times 69.625 \times 169.5)}{38{,}861 - (8 \times 69.625 \times 69.625)}$$

$$b = \frac{94{,}839 - 94{,}411.5}{38{,}861 - 38{,}781.125}$$

$$b = \frac{427.5}{79.876} = 5.352$$

a is the point where the diagonal (regression) line crosses the vertical (Y) axis. This is found from:

FIGURE 3–3 Boxed Area of Figure 3–2

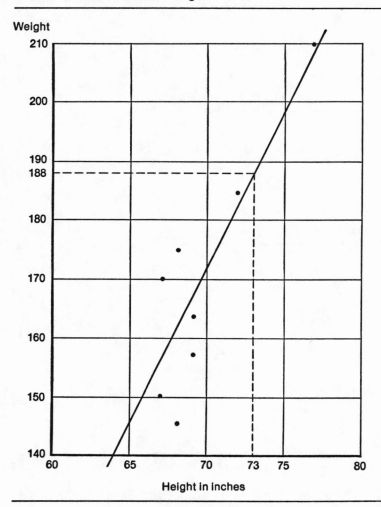

Height in inches

$$a = \bar{Y} - b\bar{X}$$

$\bar{Y}$ is the average weight (169.5), $\bar{X}$ is the average height (69.625), and we just found b for our example to be 5.352. Therefore:

$$a = 169.5 - (5.352 \times 69.625)$$

$$a = 169.5 - 372.633 = -203.133$$

The beginning algebra student learns that he can define a straight line if he knows one point on the line and the slope of the line. Thus with the constants a and b our height/weight line becomes:

$$Y = a + bX$$

$$Y = -203.133 + (5.352X)$$

By substituting any height into the equation, the corresponding weight can be found. If a person is 70 inches tall, then:

$$Y = -203.133 + (5.352 \times 70)$$

$$Y = -203.133 + 374.64 = 171.507$$

Our line predicts that this person will weigh about 171 pounds. Not perfectly accurate, because it is an imperfect relationship, but a good estimate.

How good is this relationship? The statisticians can measure the strength of the association between two variables by calculating the coefficient of determination (R^2). This is accomplished by using the totals of Table 3–3, a, b, the number of points N, and the average weight $\overline{Y}$. The formula is:

$$R^2 = \frac{aC2 + bC5 - N\overline{Y}\overline{Y}}{C4 - N\overline{Y}\overline{Y}}$$

$$R^2 = \frac{(-203.133 \times 1356) + (5.352 \times 94,839) - (8 \times 169.5 \times 169.5)}{232,970 - (8 \times 169.5 \times 169.5)}$$

$$R^2 = \frac{-275,448.34 + 507,578.32 - 229,842}{232,970 - 229,842}$$

$$R^2 = \frac{2,287.98}{3,128} = .73145$$

This number is particularly useful as it can be converted to a percentage and thus measure the percentage effect that the one variable had on the other. In our example height has a 73.145 percent effect in determining weight. The remaining 26.855 percent comes from a variety of unspecified variables, but clearly height is the dominant factor.

A perfect relationship would have an R^2 of 1.00, or 100 percent. Those with no detectable relationship would have an R^2 near zero. R can be calculated directly and is termed the correlation coefficient. This can be used to determine if the relationship is direct or inverse (Y decreases when X increases, and vice versa). The relationship is inverse if $C5 - C1 \cdot (C2/N)$ is negative. If the relationship is inverse, then R would range between 0 and -1.

Movement in gold prices and the stock indexes are usually inversely related.

An R^2 of nearly 75 percent is fairly strong in the real world and typical of money relationships. The effect of inflation on interest rates has an R^2 of nearly 75 percent. In Chapter 4 we will substitute the cost of money for P/E ratios in modeling the value of stocks, and the coefficient of determination between these two variables is 81 percent.

RETURN AND RISK

Return in the investment sense is defined as the change in market price plus any dividend paid during the period, compared to the market price at the beginning of the period. To annualize this process and measure return for more than one year, the period is normally calculated from one year-end to the next year-end, or one year in time. Table 3–4, column 2, is the year-end closing price for the Dow Jones Industrial Averages for the 15 years 1966–80. Column 3 is the total dividend paid by each component of the average. Column 4 is the change in the index from year to year. Column 5 is the sum of column 3 and column 4. Column 6 is the fractional return based on the value of the index at the end of the prior year.

For example, 149.61/785.69 = .190 for the first years return. When we sum all values in column 6 and divide by the number 14, we get the mean of .075 (7.5 percent) per year. The absolute deviation in column 7 is the difference between the mean and the fractional return of each year. The result in column 7, when multiplied by itself, will produce the variance in column 8.

Using the methods described earlier in this chapter, we find standard deviation by summing the column of variances and dividing by one less (13) than the number of values (14): .421737 ÷ 13 = .0324413. Taking the square root completes the process, giving a standard deviation of .1801147.

This means that by definition the return on the DJIA averaged 7.5 percent for the years surveyed, with about two thirds having a return in the range of −10.5 percent to +25.5 percent (7.5 percent plus or minus 18 percent).

The standard deviation is considered the measure of risk but is not particularly meaningful by itself. You can't compare risk to

TABLE 3–4 End-of-Year Dow Jones Industrial Average Data

Year	Price	Dividend	Index Change	Change + Dividend	Return	Absolute Deviation	Variance
1966	$ 785.69						
1967	905.11	$30.19	119.42	149.61	.190	.115	.013225
1968	943.75	31.34	38.64	69.98	.077	.002	.000004
1969	800.36	33.90	−143.39	−109.49	−.116	.191	.036480
1970	838.92	31.53	38.56	70.09	.088	.013	.000189
1971	890.20	30.86	51.28	82.14	.098	.023	.000529
1972	1,020.02	32.27	129.82	162.09	.182	.107	.011449
1973	850.86	35.33	−169.16	−133.83	−.131	.206	.042436
1974	616.24	37.72	−234.62	−196.90	−.231	.306	.093600
1975	852.41	37.46	236.17	273.63	.444	.369	.136160
1976	1,004.65	41.40	152.24	196.64	.231	.156	.024336
1977	831.17	45.84	−173.48	−127.64	−.127	.202	.040804
1978	805.01	48.52	−26.16	22.36	.027	.048	.002304
1979	838.74	50.98	33.73	84.71	.105	.030	.000900
1980	963.74	54.36	125.00	179.36	.214	.139	.019321

return directly, as 18 compared to 7.5 suggests nearly three times as much risk as return and implies that most stocks make a poor investment.

What is useful is the comparison of the pair of values (risk, return) to the same calculated pair in another investment. In 1952 Harry Markowitz published the seminal work on using these measures in portfolio selection to ensure the best combination of risk and return.

Beta

William Sharpe studied the effect of portfolio diversification on the risk assumed by the investor and developed a measure of the variability of a stock's price, now known as beta. The beta value measures market risk of an individual stock by comparing the returns of the stock against a market index.

Using Table 3–4 I developed a standard deviation for the DJIA for the years 1966–80. I could just as well have chosen the Standard & Poor's 500 Stock Average, the Value Line composite, or any of a number of other market indexes. If we were to construct another table with the same column headings but used the year-end closing price and dividend of an individual stock, we would get a column of yearly returns that might be compared to column 6 of Table 3–4.

Table 3–5 does compare the DJIA to the Xerox Corporation after the returns have been changed from fractional form to percentages. The standard deviation of the Xerox returns is 29.65, and the mean return is 5.6 percent. If we plot the yearly returns on a scatter diagram (as we did height and weight in Figure 3–2) with the DJIA considered the independent or causal variable, then Figure 3–4 would result. Regression analysis would result in a regression line forecasting the Xerox price percentage change, when given the percentage change of the Dow. That line would be:

$$X_p = -.86 + .85762D_p$$

where D_p is the predicted DJIA.

Remember that the basic form of the equation of a straight line is $Y = a + bX$.

If b (beta) is .85762, then it measures the slope of the regression line plotted in Figure 3–4. This value represents the market risk

TABLE 3–5 Dow Jones Industrial Average versus Xerox

Year	DJIA Percentage Return	Xerox Percentage Return
1967	19	46
1968	8	−6
1969	−12	16
1970	9	−22
1971	10	42
1972	18	30
1973	−13	−25
1974	−23	−57
1975	44	−4
1976	23	33
1977	−13	−19
1978	3	21
1979	11	23
1980	21	0

that is computed and published by a number of data services, most notably the *Value Line Investment Survey*. The standard deviations compared in a ratio measure total risk, including both the effect of the market and any factors unique to Xerox.

The total risk is 29.65/18, or 1.65. The correlation of Xerox to the DJIA is only 27 percent, showing a tendency to be fairly independent of market movement for the period studied. Complete independence would result in an R^2 near zero.

In our example, we used annual data, but monthly, weekly, or daily data could be used as long as the method chosen is consistent for all betas calculated. There will be some variation in results, depending on the method used and the time span.

Value Line adjusts the computed beta by including one part average (1) with two parts computed. The reason they do this is that most stocks tend to become more "average" as they mature and we want to look ahead. An average company will have a beta near one, while older, more established companies (like utilities) may have a beta near .5. The more volatile, younger companies have betas that may be near 2.0 in value.

The beta can be used alone in determining risk to be undertaken when purchasing a stock or can be combined with the weight of each issue in a portfolio to determine the overall portfolio

FIGURE 3–4 Dow Jones Industrials versus Xerox Return: Scatter Diagram and Regression Line

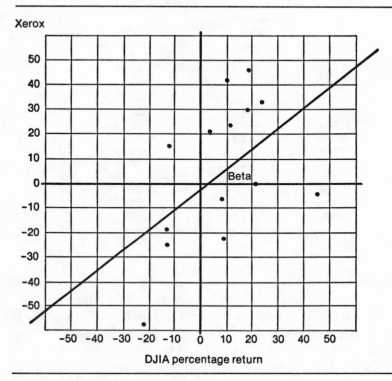

Xerox

DJIA percentage return

balance and volatility. I use it in this manner for assessing portfolio status but also use it for modeling stock value (Chapter 4) and for computing limit order prices (Chapter 5).

If you have a computer, all the processes described in this chapter are included as programs in Chapter 10.

Equity Valuation

> You accumulate a fortune by buying straw hats in January.
> —*Russell Sage*

John Houseman opens a commercial for Smith, Barney and Company by saying: "Good investments don't walk up and bite you on the bottom and say we're here!" Facetious as it may be, that is the way most investors operate. They beg the tip of friends, relatives, or their broker and then act on that recommendation with little or no investigation. They may find out what the company produces, but rarely will they spend as much time in selecting stocks as they do in buying a car—or a lawnmower, for that matter.

Ross Perot, the dynamic president of Electronic Data Systems was asked how he recruited such good people. His reply was, "Eagles don't flock—you have to find them one at a time." Stocks are the same way—to find value, you have to do some work.

The question that requires an answer is, "What is it worth?" If you were to buy a house, you certainly would seek that answer. You'd look at recent sales in the neighborhood, measure the lot and the floor space, and check taxes and neighbors' opinions until you had an idea of value. You'd then offer on that basis.

If you were buying a business, there would be even more of an investigation to determine worth. You would estimate inventory, look at gross revenue, and itemize assets and liabilities to determine a net worth.

Stocks must be analyzed the same way. Pretend you're buying the entire company and do what you would do in that circumstance. It shouldn't matter whether you buy 1 million shares or 1 share. There is intrinsic value to be determined.

WHERE DO WE START?

Where do you find the stocks? The answer is all around you. The universe of some 10,000 stocks should be reduced to the few companies that you are already well informed about.

Rather than systematically searching all stocks on selected mechanical criteria (screening), I only buy stocks that meet one of the following conditions:

1. They are companies that I have worked for or done business with.
2. They are located nearby.
3. They produce a product that I am familiar with as a professional.
4. Their product is well known, and its appeal is easy to understand.

In my case this limits possibilities to less than 100 stocks. As an exercise, you might list all the companies that you know that meet one of these requirements.

If your list has as many as 10 candidates, then you should have enough choice to play the game successfully. With this many stocks, one or two should be good prospects at any time. I buy and sell the same stocks over and over. In Chapter 8, I'll describe my first purchase of Control Data in 1963. I bought it again in 1966, and it was all that I had after the savings and loan fiasco mentioned in the Preface to this book. I sold it short in 1968 (described in Chapter 7) and have recently started to buy it again. You might say that I buy and sell Control Data.

First let's put the stock selection topic in perspective. It is by far the most overrated aspect of good investment practice. I could do nearly as well if my selections had been made by a monkey (or a broker) with a dart. It's not how you pick them—it's how you play them!

The advantage of knowing the stocks that you select is that it creates an information base that serves you well during future random events. You're not nearly so likely to panic if you understand the implications of a new piece of information.

Start with *Value Line Investment Survey* data. Your local library or the brokerage firm should be able to produce a recent fact sheet. If no Value Line, use Standard & Poor's or Moody's. Learn the company's business, earnings, price history, and problems. It's all there.

The more familiar the company, the easier the backgrounding process. If you know the companies, you're much more likely to find the ones with potential and bear with them while they develop.

Most stocks are going to be fairly priced, based on current information. After all, there are a buyer and a seller. You have to look for "overdone" or "underdeveloped" situations and then be bold in their acquisition.

THE TRAVELING COMPANIONS: DISTRESS AND OPPORTUNITY

The Chinese symbols for danger and for opportunity are the same. The more risk you're willing to accept, the more potential reward.

Bargain-priced stocks fall into two categories: troubled or unknown! If company prospects are good and well known, then the stock will be priced at or above value. Market price is determined by earnings or *anticipated* earnings during prosperity and by net asset value in hard times. The shrewd investor concentrates on larger (quality) companies in periods of unpopularity created by depressed earnings or poor market conditions.

Benjamin Graham, the leading investment analyst of this century, wrote in *The Intelligent Investor* the following:

> If we can assume that it is the habit of the market to overvalue common stocks which have been showing excellent growth or are glamorous for some other reason, it is logical to expect that it will undervalue—relatively at least—companies that are out of favor because of unsatisfactory developments of a temporary nature. This may be set down as a fundamental law of the stock market, and it suggests an investment approach that should prove most conservative and promising.
>
> The key requirement here is that the enterprising investor concentrate on the larger companies that are going through a period of unpopularity.

This should immediately suggest some guidelines for the investment process. I would identify the following three as starters:

1. Don't buy stocks that have had a recent run-up in price. This represents a psychological inflation that presents little opportunity.
2. Don't buy stocks that are excessively active, even if it is to the downside. Wait for the "dullness" that suggests that

the market has lost interest in the company and its problems. Major movements begin in dullness and end in dullness.

3. Don't buy a stock that is priced in multiples of book value. No bargain here!

The analysis deals with the answers to these questions:

1. What is the company currently worth?
2. What are the problems creating the markdown in share prices?
3. Are these problems correctable, and when?
4. To what level of earnings will the company return in prosperity?

If recovery is questionable, then turn your attention elsewhere. You'll probably get caught occasionally, even using extreme caution, but don't invite trouble by getting involved with companies that are over the brink.

VALUE IN GOOD TIMES AND BAD

In times of prosperity for a company, the earnings per share or anticipated earnings will be the principal determinant of share price. If you can tell me what a company will earn during the next fiscal year, I can quote you a price that will be met sometime during that year.

Of course, determining what those earnings will be is difficult, even though the quest is pursued by the best minds in the business. If the earnings are predictable, then the pricing will follow, with no real bargain to be had. If the consensus of earnings estimates is optimistic, then the stock will become overvalued, resulting in a jarring adjustment in price when the actual results are known.

If the company is having problems, then the earnings estimates becomes progressively more pessimistic and the stock quickly becomes undervalued. With little or no earning prospects, the price becomes supported by net asset value (book value) of the company. Book value is not a certain parameter, as company assessment of assets may not reflect the true market worth of each individual property. Nevertheless, market price of common stock tends to stabilize near book value, even in periods of negative earnings.

If the problems are terminal, then they may erode the assets as the company tries to save itself. In this case there is no bottom to price, and what begins as a bargain ends up a disaster.

Before you buy troubled stocks, perform the following analysis:

1. How realistic is the reported book value of the company? Would the assets be attractive to another company?
2. Has cash flow slowed down to where the debt burden will consume assets voraciously? Is the quick ratio below 1?
3. Is inventory piling up and possibly not marketable at all? Is there a product that is ready for the market that will be acceptable?
4. Is the company cutting expenses and adjusting to competition? Does their appraisal of the situation seem realistic?
5. Is the current trouble resultant from a poor economy? Can improvement be expected?

If you can see beyond the current troubles, a depressed stock offers maximum opportunity. Ideally you would like one that could turn around the difficulty in a year's time and return to earnings levels reached before the trouble began. Current market price could be compared to prior price levels, or prior earnings could be used to model value under prosperous conditions.

The other possibility for significant price gain is the undeveloped or unknown company. This would describe most over-the-counter stocks, many of which have only a dream to build on.

Once an earnings stream is established it may be possible to estimate earnings one to three years ahead and model value accordingly. This is most difficult though; everyone else likes to play this game, which tends to keep the current market price on the optimistic side. I've done much better by looking for the larger, established companies that are temporarily out of favor.

The one thing that is virtually certain is that the company with rosy prospects which is invoking recommendations from all quarters will not make much money for you and likely will create large losses.

Only the outcasts can be bargains. Buy the ones that have had drastic markdowns in price and are being "bad-mouthed" by the investment community, but be alert to that fine line between bargain and disaster.

MAXIM 4–1 Value is determined by earnings in prosperity and book value in adversity.

The Cost of Money

Love may make the world go around, but it is money that greases the wheels. The availability of money can cause prosperity or depression.

Wealth is continually changing hands, sometimes available in oversupply and other times scarce. The price of use (borrowing) varies with the available supply.

When we hold money, we will move it to receive what we perceive as the best return, given a certain level of risk aversion. If we can get good results from bonds or certificates of deposit, we'll pull money from the stock market in seeking higher fixed return. Conversely, when fixed rates fall, money is returned to equities in search of relatively higher returns.

The measure of return from the stock market is normally growth plus dividend yield, but a more stable measure is earnings yield (see Chapter 3). Earnings yield represents the actual total profit production on the market value of the common shares. It is logical that earnings yield should vary as the cost of money varies. When money is expensive the earnings yield should be relatively high. That means that company earnings are exceptional or that share prices have been lowered, resulting in a larger ratio. Since the price-earnings (P/E) ratio is the inverse of the earnings yield (E/P), the P/E ratio will be reduced when the cost of money is relatively high.

The cost of money is determined by four factors:

1. *Inflation.* During inflationary times money becomes less valuable in purchasing power, and consequently a higher use fee (interest rate) must be assessed in order to maintain value in terms of real assets. A number of statistical studies have shown the direct relationship between inflation and the cost of money. These have all produced correlations (R^2) near 75 percent, demonstrating that change in inflation causes 75 percent of the change in interest rates.

2. *Risk factors.* The amount of risk is determined by the agency issuing the paper. The federal government is considered risk free on a scale that would consider small businesses with little asset value as having maximum risk. Long-term bond yields might range from 10 to 20 percent on that basis. That means as much as 10 percent could be attributed to risk alone.

3. *Real rate of return.* After consideration of inflation expectation and the amount of risk involved, there must be a residual

FIGURE 4–1 Determinants of Market Interest Rates

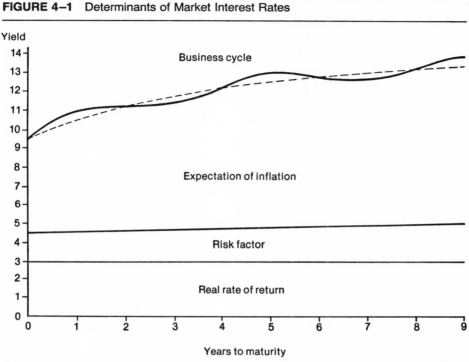

real rate of return. Historically this has been 3 to 4 percent. In times of low or no inflation a risk-free investment yields a near real rate of return. Short-term Treasury bonds are considered risk free and constitute a base measure of the cost of money. Currently 90-day Treasury bills are priced to yield 6.6 percent at a time when inflation is being measured at 3.7 percent. This suggests a real rate of return of 2.9 percent.

4. *Business cycle.* The short-term demand for money by businesses will create minor fluctuations in rates as immediate needs come and go.

Figure 4–1 illustrates how these factors accumulate to create a current market rate of interest.

Assuming that a relationship exists between the cost of money and the earnings yield of the stock market, I constructed the data of Table 4–1. Since stock prices, earnings, and inflation all vary continuously, I used averages for each year. The cost of money

TABLE 4–1 Inflation versus Dow Jones Industrials (DJI) Earnings Yield

Year	Inflation (I)	Inflation + 3 percent	Dow Jones Industrials				Earnings	E/P†
			High (DJI$_h$)‡	Low (DJI$_l$)‡	Average* (DJI$_a$)‡			
1966	2.9%	5.9%	995	744	869.5		$ 57.68	6.63
1967	2.9	5.9	943	786	864.5		53.87	6.23
1968	4.2	7.2	985	825	905		57.89	6.39
1969	5.4	8.4	968	769	868.5		57.02	6.57
1970	5.9	8.9	842	631	736.5		57.02	7.74
1971	4.3	7.3	950	797	873.5		55.09	6.31
1972	3.3	6.3	1,036	889	962.5		67.11	6.97
1973	6.2	9.2	1,051	788	919.5		86.17	9.37
1974	11.0	14.0	891	577	734		99.04	13.50
1975	9.1	12.1	881	632	756.5		75.66	10.00
1976	5.8	8.8	1,014	858	936		96.72	10.33
1977	6.7	9.7	999	800	899.5		89.10	9.90
1978	7.7	10.7	907	742	824.5		112.79	13.68
1979	11.3	14.3	897	796	846.5		124.46	14.70
1980	13.5	16.5	1,000	759	879.5		121.86	13.86
1981	10.3	13.3	1,024	875	949.5		113.71	11.98

*DJI$_a$ = (DJI$_l$ + DJI$_h$)/2
†E/P = Earnings/DJI$_a$
NOTE: E/P$_f$ = (1.22228 + .849233) · (I$_f$ + 3), f is forecast
    R^2 = .8088, or 81 percent due to inflation
‡h, l, and a refer to high, low, and average.

FIGURE 4–2   Earnings/Price Ratio as a Function of Inflation, 1966–1981

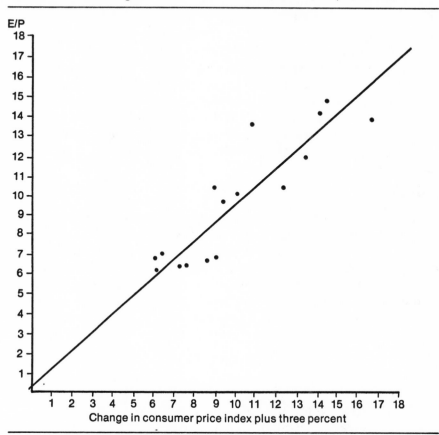

was assumed to be inflation plus 3 percent and was arbitrarily chosen because I had data for the consumer price index for the period examined. A better study might be conducted using the average 90-day Treasury bill rate for the same years.

The change in the consumer price index plus 3 percent was compared to the Dow Jones Industrial Average earnings yields for the same years. This relationship is shown in Figure 4–2. It is fairly obvious that as inflation increases, so does earnings yield (which means that P/E ratios fall). What's more, it does it in near perfect proportions. The R^2 is .8088, which is about the same relationship found by other studies of money and inflation.

I realize that my data sample is small and lacking statistical confidence; but considering the logic, it has to pique your interest. The conclusion is that in order to determine proper market level in the future, we need only to forecast the cost of money and from that compute the expected level of prices to earnings.

Predicting interest rates is still a formidable chore, but at least we can examine current market levels in relation to current interest rates to see if the market is above or below value.

Applying this relationship to individual stocks, in concert with an adjustment for the company's growth prospects, will allow us to model the stock's intrinsic value, as we shall see.

Earnings

In looking for bargains, we're planning for stocks currently priced at half what their intrinsic value will be when earnings are restored to normal levels. Obviously we have to be correct in our estimates of potential earnings, if desired price levels are to develop.

If we have a good estimate of earnings, then value of an average stock can be computed, using the average price-earnings ratio, multiplied by the earnings expected. This can be expressed in formula form:

$$V = EM$$

where:

E = Expected annual earnings per share for the year.
M = Average price-earnings multiple.
V = Intrinsic value of the stock in dollars.

IBM is an average stock. Today earnings estimates for 1985 are around $10 per share for IBM. The average price-earnings ratio for all stocks is about 12 to 1: Twelve dollars in price for each dollar of earnings. Anticipating $10 of earnings per share relates to a $120 market value. IBM sells in that neighborhood today. The only way IBM could be even a minor bargain is for significantly unexpected earnings gains to occur or for all stocks to be in demand, raising the average price-earnings ratio beyond 12.

What should the average price-earnings ratio be today? Is 12 appropriate for a stock with normal prospects for future growth in earnings? Twelve for a P/E indicates an earnings yield of 8.3 percent (12:1 becomes 1:12 or .083).

Figure 4–2 demonstrates that the market averages have an earnings yield near the risk-free rate of return. Today that is near 7 percent, so 8.3 percent implies that the P/E ratio is a little low for current circumstances. Seven percent is a P/E of 14 to 1.

The larger ratio could be met through poorer earnings, as many economists are predicting recession, or it could be met by improved stock prices. If interest rates and/or inflation were to increase, then the P/E would be restricted or would begin adjusting to lower levels.

Obviously, forecasting is not a simple problem, because of the mixture of variables, the difficulty of assessing each, and the market psychology that tends to anticipate or ignore changes of each.

However, on a probability basis, we can look at apparent extremes and adjust our activity accordingly. In 1982 I was fairly certain that a major reversal was in prospect and became fully margined. Today I'm not sure of anything but believe that the odds favor a continued rise in stock prices. Therefore I'm not invested to the point of vulnerability but have all my own funds committed with an additional 20 percent use of margin. If the Dow advances another 100 points (1,400 +), then I'll give up the margin and move toward more conservative investments with my own money. I have been "in the market" continuously since my savings and loan episode in 1966.

Adjustment for Growth

Graham said in *The Intelligent Investor:* "The appraised value is determined by estimating the earnings power, applying thereto a suitable multiplier, and adjusting if necessary for asset value."

I hope that I've been convincing in stating that earnings are the single most important determinant of stock prices and that the cost of money is sufficiently related to price-earnings multiples that substitution may be made to determine appropriate value.

The third factor, adjustment for value or growth, is more difficult, and even as great an analyst as Graham was not very convincing in his computation.

Let's examine the problem logically. Some stocks have greater expectations than others and should command a higher price-earnings ratio than average. You are willing to defer current earnings and dividends derived therefrom, until the potential can be fully realized. Thus dynamic new companies with glowing prospects may deserve ratios of 20, 25, or even 30 to 1. The question is, "What is the correct ratio for this stock?"

Many successful stock market advisors select only low P/E stocks. I have no doubt that it can be a successful strategy, but it automatically eliminates over half of the stocks. We can open up your prospects to a wider circle of candidates if we can judge what a relatively low P/E ratio is for stocks with differing growth prospects. How do we measure the growth possibility?

Growth in earnings comes immediately to mind. Certainly the public at large is conditioned to statements about earnings growing at X percent per year. Use for forecasting, however, is tricky because the rate varies widely from year to year and, if consistent, will be already reflected in share prices. Return on equity is more predictable but still of little use in periods of reduced earnings, which is where we seek opportunity.

This type of examine-and-discard reasoning led me to the market risk (volatility) factor beta. Beta is relatively stable and logically should reflect company prospects. *Better prospects warrant higher risk!* Certainly the newer companies, yet to be proven, have higher market risk than the older, stabler concerns.

Beta has some other advantages: It is in ratio form, related to the average stock (beta of 1), and immediately useful without adjustment. It is readily available from Value Line in a diluted form (which makes estimates more conservative) or can be easily computed from recent price changes.

The caveat is that the data is historical and may not be representative of the period of time in which you intend to use it. However, what do you have that is better, and where can you find any guarantees concerning the markets? If it works 51 percent of the time, it will be useful.

Consulting my shopping list during this investigation of models, I plotted beta versus price-earnings ratios on a scatter diagram. A correlational analysis produced an R^2 of near .50. The sample was small (16) and had been selected on fundamentals, but these results extended my interest. I next picked some random samples of 100–300 stocks and ran correlations on each sample. Again a mild relationship existed. I monitored the progress of my 16 stocks over the next year, finding a slight correlation of percentage price change to the overvalued/undervalued status according to beta.

The evidence for using beta as an adjustment factor for growth is logical but tenuous. However, the entire forecasting process is shaky—certainly no better than the estimated earnings. Still a poor relationship is better than none at all in an imperfect world where any statistical edge is desirable.

MAXIM 4–2   Select stocks with low P/E and high beta.

Value Models

How do we know where a stock should be priced? The broker will tell you that this is a $50 stock selling for $30. Does he base his $50 price on expected earnings of $5 next year and a P/E ratio of 10? If so, he has devised a simple mathematical model, an attempt to simplify and simulate reality. In this case he has reduced all the factors weighing on the price of a stock to expected earnings and his perception of a proper P/E ratio for that stock.

Economists and investment analysts are constantly seeking models that will allow them to forecast interest rates and stock prices. Models for bonds, options, and other fixed maturity–based securities are fairly efficient, as there are fewer variables, a fixed time frame, and a known result. The present value of a bond can be calculated as accurately as your vision of average interest rates for the holding period. Stocks are much more complicated.

Most of the stock pricing models used in academic circles deal with discounting the future stream of dividends to be received on the stock. These require adjustments for the amount of dividend yield, growth rate, etc., and are of little value as a practical tool for the individual investor.

So why try to produce a forecasting model, when the finest minds have thus far failed to improve on random selection? Because there is logic behind stock pricing, and that logic can be calculated with mathematics. Not perfectly, as the psychology will override the logic just as mountain effects override the equations of motion in weather prediction, but any insight at all may reduce your losses by 1 in 100 and will thus be worthwhile.

We start with the three variables proposed by Graham and make the substitutions that I suggest:

1. Annual earnings per share (E).
2. Price-earnings multiples (M) as determined by risk-free cost of money (C).
3. Adjust P/E for growth (K), using beta (b).

Graham's value model is $V = EMK$. Making the substitutions $M = 1/C$ and $K = b$, where C is the cost of money and b is beta, $V = E \cdot (1/C) \cdot b$, and simplifying gives Sharp's value model:

$$V = E \cdot \frac{b}{C}$$

The substitutions allow use of more stable, readily available parameters. Earnings should be a consensus, slightly defensive or conservative, using a variety of sources. Beta can be *Value Line Investment Survey* data (conservative) or calculated. The cost of money can be Treasury bill rate, federal reserve discount rate, or inflation plus 3 percent, depending on which you feel is most representative at the moment. The model admittedly is not perfect and should be used judiciously. You may want to experiment with using other variables as substitutes for the ones that I have chosen.

Example: The utility stocks have been in demand recently, and Dominion Resources came from a low of 20.375 in 1984 to a current high near 33. The expected earnings per share for 1985 is $3.60. Value Line beta is .6, and the Treasury bill rate is 6.7 percent.

The model price (value) of Dominion Resources under these conditions is:

$$V = 3.60 \times \frac{.6}{.067} = 32.24$$

This is close to where the stock is currently trading, and the price represents full value. No bargain here, but last year it was, had we foreseen how low the interest rate level would drop.

On the other hand, General Motors expects earnings in excess of $12 per share for 1985. With a beta of 1.1, value is:

$$V = 12 \cdot \frac{1.1}{.067} = 197$$

Priced near 72 currently, it appears to be the bargain we seek, provided the estimated earnings become actuals. Obviously the market foresees a recession for the American automobile industry and has priced the stock accordingly. The stock will pay a 7 percent dividend while you wait for the issue to be resolved.

Using the model. The model may point out under/overvalued situations that could continue in that state for years. The market psychology has to be right to move price, even if the fundamentals are in place. The principal use of the model is in discovering potential and guarding against significant loss.

If you buy a stock that appears to be at half value, there is no guarantee that anything will change. It may stay at that level for years, but it is unlikely to move significantly lower unless the entire market comes under pressure.

The principal advantage to the model is allowing you to avoid issues that are apparently overpriced. I buy only those stocks that are priced at 50 percent or less of model value. The half-price benchmark is chosen because less than 10 percent of the stocks fall into that category. A stock selected from this group is more likely to join the other 90 percent than it is to go lower in price.

Also I proposed in Chapter 1 that you seek 100 percent potential in order to capitalize on the exponential movement of stock prices. The average New York Stock Exchange stock trades as much as 60 percent above its low during a typical year, so there are plenty of stocks that make a 100 percent gain.

You play the statistics, and that means being disciplined enough to buy only as long as you model value at half-price. If price moves above the 50 percent level, discontinue any further purchases.

MAXIM 4–3   Buy quality companies at half-value.

The model should only be used to buy. If you own a stock that appreciates into the overvalued state, you shouldn't be in any hurry to sell it. Things usually get overdone in both directions, so it may become as overvalued as it was undervalued earlier (see Chapter 5 on selling). The idea is that you not buy fully valued stocks.

The model doesn't provide any clear-cut answers. The choices are never obvious. That's why there is a market that promotes both buying and selling. Use the model for guidance only and not as absolute authority.

Portfolio Management

Traditional diversification is the Noah's Ark approach—You buy two of
everything in sight and end up with a zoo instead of a portfolio.
—*Warren Buffett*

To paraphrase Warren Buffett, traditional diversification guarantees mediocrity. The only consistent piece of advice offered by
all investment gurus is that of diversification. It is a rational, considered, and wise recommendation that couldn't be more wrong.

One adviser will recommend a minimum of 10 stocks; a second
adviser will recommend 20. The first will suggest a minimum
$10,000 portfolio, the second $100,000. Since 85 percent of working people have less than $5,000 to invest, the end of the adviser's
logic chain is to suggest a mutual fund. Mutual funds, on average,
haven't done as well over time as the Dow Jones Industrial Averages.

The above reasoning should lead one to the conclusion that
you should not invest in stocks. At today's interest levels, a certificate of deposit or a long-term Treasury (or corporate) bond
will guarantee a rate that beats historical market indexes. If rates
go higher tomorrow or next year, you will regret buying the fixed-income instrument, but you would have regretted buying stock,
under those circumstances.

The focus of the advisers is on risk rather than on return. By
protecting against significant loss, they advise against significant
reward and in effect negate the principal advantage of the stock
market—capital-appreciation potential.

I'm a basketball fan, and I think there is an investment analogy
there: Time after time, a basketball team will play wide open,
racehorse-type basketball to build up a comfortable lead and then
will turn conservative to protect the lead. As often as not, they
will lose the game because of their careful tactics.

The wide-open game will create some mistakes, but these will be balanced or exceeded by brilliant play. So must the investor approach the market with an aggressive, positive form of play.

THERE'S NO FREE LUNCH

There are no risk-free investments. There are some without recognizable risk, but it exists to some degree in all investments. Even if you bury gold in the proverbial tin can, you run the risk of deflation, discovery, or memory loss.

Hard assets, such as real estate, have the risk of uninsured loss and poor or no market when you're ready to sell. In addition you're taxed on face value and pay insurance premiums against more common risks.

Currency of any form depends on the stability of the agency issuing the certificate and the depreciating effect of inflation on its purchasing power.

So the paramount market truth is that reward expected from investment is directly proportional to inherent risk. If big rewards are promised, big risk is involved. It is not for the investor to decide if he will accept risk, it is simply how much to accept! There is no free lunch! Sooner or later you pay for the reward you seek, in terms of risk.

The theoretical relationship between return and risk is called the capital market line. This is a linear relationship that expects a direct increase in risk as you seek more return in an investment. See Figure 5–1. The points represent individual investments.

The academics measure risk as the deviation on change of price from year to year, but this doesn't translate to odds on total loss of your fund. Banks and savings and loans would appear to the left on the risk/reward, or capital market, line; but my father had his locked up in the bank holiday of 1933, and mine went the same route in 1966. This immediately puts risk into perspective and was key to my aggressive strategy and success in stocks.

I believe that a properly diversified portfolio of fundamentally sound common stocks, while having the illusion of high risk, really is a low-risk investment.

Market versus Unique Risk

The risk element in an individual stock can be broken into two components: the market influence and the net result of all unique factors weighing on the company.

FIGURE 5–1   The Capital Market Line

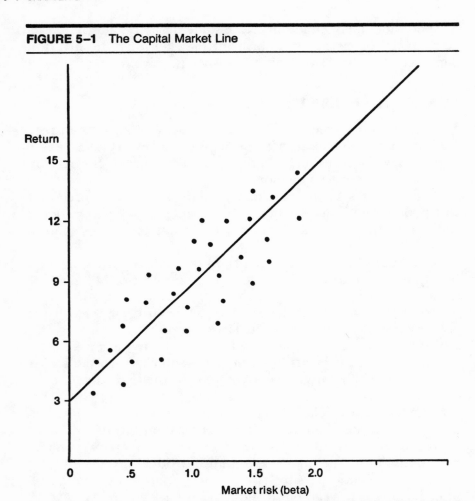

The market, or systematic, risk is measured by the beta factor described in Chapter 3. The unique, or unsystematic, risk can be determined by comparing total risk with market risk. Total risk is calculated by the ratio of the individual stock's standard deviation to the market's standard deviation for the same time period.

Diversification, if carried far enough, will eliminate the effect of unique risk. The stocks with good news will offset the ones with

FIGURE 5–2 Risk Vectors

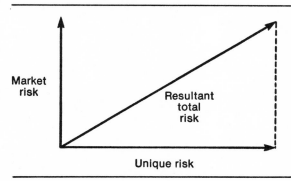

bad influences, leaving only the economy and the psychology of the market to determine portfolio direction.

The most important point (rarely made) is that diversification has no effect on the market risk component, other than guaranteeing it. That is why the mutual funds go up and down so violently even though there are hundreds of stocks in their portfolios.

On balance, the market risk component is much more likely to cause trouble than the unique factor—you're more likely to be hurt by market movement than by anything troubling each of the companies in your portfolio.

The two forces of market risk and unique risk could be represented as force vectors and analyzed as a physicist might study other force-related phenomena. A simpler method might be to eliminate the direction of the force and consider the relative or absolute strength of each component.

The two forces can act in concert, lining up their effect to force a stock up or down, or they may work in opposition. For example: good news on a company may override a falling market. However, since we don't know which direction either will take in advance, we can consider only their absolute relative importance by plotting each as working in independent directions 90 degrees apart. Figure 5–2 illustrates.

The resultant vector is the total force exerted on the stock as a combination of both market and unique factors. Using the Xerox

FIGURE 5–3 Xerox Risk Triangle

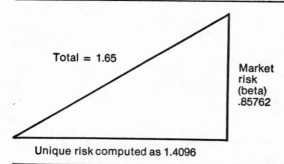

Total = 1.65

Market
risk
(beta)
.85762

Unique risk computed as 1.4096

example in Chapter 3, with a total risk of 1.65 and a market risk (beta) of .85762 we can determine the amount of unique force previously demonstrated in the stock.

Since the forces are working at right angles (90 degrees) to each other, we can use the relationship discovered by the Greek mathematician Pythagoras, over 2,500 years ago.

The Pythagorean theorem states that the three sides of a right triangle are related as follows: The longest side (hypotenuse) when multiplied by itself (squared) generates a number that is equal to the sum of the squares of the other two sides. This means that knowing two sides of a right triangle allows calculation of the third. In our example the hypotenuse is the total risk (T) of 1.65. The market risk (M) of .85762 represents one of the two remaining sides (see Figure 5–3). Substitution of these numbers in the Pythagorean theorem will allow the unique (U) factor to be determined.

$$T^2 = M^2 + U^2$$

$$U^2 = T^2 - M^2$$

$$U^2 = (1.65 \times 1.65) - (.85762 \times .85762)$$

$$U^2 = 2.7225 - .735512 = 1.986988$$

$$U^2 = \sqrt{1.986988} = 1.4096$$

In this example the unique factor has had a greater effect on price behavior than the market during the years surveyed. It happened to be a period of time when the Japanese were very competitive in the copier industry and exerted a negative influence on Xerox, overriding the market ups and downs.

The total risk describes how volatile the stock is, in terms of deviation compared to average market deviation. The market risk describes the amount of this deviation due to the market alone, where a value of one is average. The unique factor is the relative force of market-independent factors unique to the stock under study.

These factors can be managed in a portfolio in the following way: The amount of market risk (volatility) sought in candidates can be less in vulnerable markets and more when market conditions appear to be favorable. This can be done by monitoring the beta of stocks added or dropped from the portfolio. Stocks can be selected that are not highly correlated—that may, in fact, have a history of opposition in price movement. They can also be correlated with or against the market. As mentioned earlier, just increasing the number of issues in your portfolio effectively cancels out the unique factors as an average balance of good and bad emerges.

Most of the investment risk can be properly managed in the portfolio creation phase by:

1. Choosing the proper number of issues.
2. Ensuring independence of price movement in each.
3. Staggering entry into each over time.

OPTIMAL NUMBER OF ISSUES

Canceling out the unique factor of risk by diversification protects you from the negative aspects, but it also prevents you from benefiting by the positive things that might occur in any one company. If your portfolio contains an infinite number of stocks, then it must behave as a market index does. Indexing is promoted as something good; but how can it be, as the record for indexes has been so mediocre.

Andrew Carnegie said, "I determined that the proper policy was to put all good eggs in one basket and then watch that basket. I have no faith in the policy of scattering one's resources, and in my experience I have rarely, if ever, met a man who achieved

FIGURE 5–4   Risk as a Function of Portfolio Size

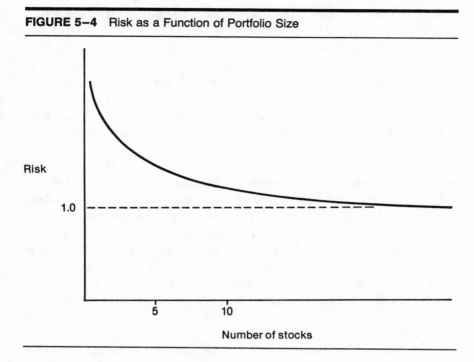

preeminence in money-making who was interested in many concerns."[1]

You can't ignore the unique risk factor entirely, but you should seek enough risk to promote near-maximum potential of the portfolio.

Figure 5–4 shows how approximately 75 percent of the unique risk is eliminated in a portfolio of five randomly chosen stocks. Five stocks in the same industry group wouldn't behave much differently from one or two taken from the group (assuming the financial parameters are sound), and five chosen carefully with poor statistical correlation would have virtually no unique portfolio risk and would also compensate somewhat against market risk. Since we have reasons other than statistical correlation to consider in stock selection, we might consider Figure 5–4 to be representative.

---

[1]Andrew Carnegie, *Autobiography of Andrew Carnegie* (Boston: Houghton-Mifflin, 1920).

Let's digress for a moment and consider what we are trying to protect against. The ultimate threat is personal bankruptcy, and we should take reasonable precautions against this possibility. We can't eliminate the possibility entirely, regardless of the number of stocks held, but it quickly becomes unlikely after the addition of a second stock to your portfolio.

Unless you're playing penny stocks, the chances of buying a stock that eventually becomes worthless is less than 1 in 100. The process of depreciating value usually requires years to accomplish, with reorganization under Chapter 11 bankruptcy law or purchase by another company possible. Disciplined investment using the short-term tax loss provision will let you out with less than total loss.

Still, it can happen; and whether it is total loss or significant (50 percent or more), the setback to a one-stock portfolio would require years to recover. The chances are that you'll probably encounter at least one of these "alligators" during your investing career.

Now let's consider a two-stock portfolio. If each stock has less than a 1 percent chance of total loss, then the portfolio probability of total loss is less than 1 chance in 10,000 (.01 × .01). Of course total loss in one stock still would reduce portfolio value by 50 percent. This assumes the investment fund is equally divided across all stocks in the portfolio.

MAXIM 5–1 Balance your portfolio with near equal amounts in all stocks.

My first 100 trades charted in Figure 1–6 indicate one loss of near 90 percent and eight others of 50 percent or greater. The worst loss was a real "crapshoot" that I had no business owning and refused to sell, long after the handwriting was on the wall. The dollar amount was less than 5 percent of my portfolio, but I violated most of my own principles.

The 50 percent losses are a real threat and must be managed. In a two-stock portfolio, one of these reduces portfolio value by 25 percent, which represents a one-year setback. However this should occur less than 10 percent of the time, and getting two in the same portfolio occurs less than 1 in 100 times. Bad markets will also set your portfolio back by 25 percent or more, and this will occur approximately once every four years.

The logical conclusion to this evidence, based on my record, is that a two-stock portfolio, reasonably selected, can expect less damage from unique factors than from a poor general market.

However, my record, selection, emotions, and the money that I have at risk are different from your situation, so how can you determine what your optimal portfolio size should be?

It is my contention that the individual investor should never have less than two stocks in his portfolio, nor should he have more than five. The precise number may be calculated based on his past record and hedged upward into his emotional comfort zone, depending on the amount at risk and the utility that it represents. Nevertheless there is very little to be gained in extending the portfolio beyond five stocks.

I realize this is heresy, but I know what I've accomplished with three stocks or less in my portfolio, and luck has had nothing to do with it. It's a simple case of statistics.

Statisticians have long been intrigued with bet-sizing and setting defense against "gambler's ruin" (complete loss of bankroll). Some of the best mathematicians from Blaise Pascal to John Von Neumann have worked the problem.

More recently, Edward Thorpe of the University of California at Irvine, who initiated the card-counting strategies in blackjack (*Beat the Dealer*) and warrant strategies (*Beat the Market*), has published research on bet-sizing applied to warrants and options.

The problem is how to reduce the risk of bankruptcy while capitalizing the expected net successes. This assumes that the game has a positive mathematical expectation, the bankroll is large enough to be subdivided into reasonable bet units, and the expected statistical results are known.

Betting the correct fraction of current bankroll is the key, and proper bet-sizing has been formulated as the optimal-betting principle. This is a two-step process:

1. Calculate the payoff odds, using the probability formula $(p \cdot X) - (q \cdot 1) = R$.
2. Use Kelly's strategy, which is expected return divided by the payoff odds.

p is the probability (fraction) of success, q is the probability of failure ($p + q = 1$), and R is the expected fraction of return. X is payoff odds.

This strategy has been applied to race track betting, as demonstrated in the following example:

A person picking winners 36 percent of the time (.36) yielding 26 percent return (.26) would on average have payoff odds of 2.5 to 1. This comes from:

$$(p \cdot X) - (q \cdot 1) = R$$

$$.36X - (.64 \cdot 1) = .26$$

$$.36X = .90$$

$$X = 2.5$$

Kelly's strategy says that the 26 percent return as a fraction (.26), divided by the payoff odds (2.5) suggests a bankroll fraction of .104, or slightly more than 10 percent on each race.

If we apply this strategy to the stock market, then a very conservative estimate of number of stocks to be held might emerge.

Employing algebra, the two formulas may be combined and rearranged to spcify the number of stocks (N):

$$N = \frac{R + q}{R \cdot p}$$

Using an example of a person picking winners 50 percent of the time for a net 10 percent return would specify a 12-stock portfolio.

$$N = \frac{.10 + .50}{.10 \times .50} = \frac{.60}{.05} = 12$$

This is conservative, as it is based on gambling games where a loss is total loss of the unit bet. Since stock losses are usually partial the formula would be more realistic if modified to accept the expected average percentage loss of each losing investment. If our average percentage loss is 25 percent (mine is 27 percent), then we are apparently dealing with 48 units (12/.25) rather than 12 that could be 100 percent losses. Modifying the formula for the losing fraction (L) gives:

$$N = L\left(\frac{R + q}{R \cdot p}\right) = .25 \cdot \left(\frac{.60}{.05}\right) = 3$$

This example suggesting a three-stock portfolio should be representative of the average investor. If a person hasn't traded enough to establish his parameters, then he would do well to consider a three-stock portfolio as standard until such time when his ability is proven.

MAXIM 5–2   A speculative portfolio for the average investor should contain three stocks unless his record, emotions, or total amount at risk dictates adjustment.

INDEPENDENCE OF PRICE MOVEMENT

It is not enough to accept my premise of three stocks with near-equal dollar amounts in each. You must be concerned that the stocks are not look-alikes, and you must also know whether the stock has a history of moving in harmony with the general market averages or counter to market trends.

The mathematical process that allows us to determine these relationships is correlation analysis, described in "Statistical Measures," Chapter 3. Fund managers use this analysis to specify how much of the total fund should be allocated to each stock to maximize the ratio of reward to risk. The combining process is termed Markowitz diversification. This is of little use to the individual, as he can't diversify to the extent that a fund may. The individual should be concerned with the historical relationship of the candidates. Once selection has been made, funds should be split equally among the selected stocks.

The process does use historical data, and the future price action may not correspond to the past. There are no guarantees! However, on a probability basis, taking this precaution should make your portfolio much less vulnerable to random market disasters.

In the Xerox example of Chapter 3 the computed R^2 was 27 percent. This represents a stock that is fairly independent of market movement. The computation can range between 0 and 100 percent so anything below 50 percent is more independent than correlated to the stock or index used for comparison.

If you think the market will be exceptionally good, then you may want to select a stock with a high (near 100 percent) correlation with the appropriate market index.

Most of the time you'll probably do well to compare stocks to be added to the portfolio against stocks already owned to ensure

TABLE 5-1 Annual Percentage Return

Year	Texaco	Exxon	United Airlines	Dow Industrials
1969	−29.6%	−20.3%	−34.1%	−11.6
1970	34.3	26.3	−18.8	8.8
1971	10.0	5.3	86.4	9.8
1972	9.6	27.5	−12.2	18.2
1973	−25.7	9.4	−44.4	−13.1
1974	−17.5	−29.3	−26.8	−23.1
1975	23.8	55.0	104.3	44.4
1976	25.0	24.4	2.1	23.1
1977	3.6	−2.0	−26.4	−12.7
1978	−3.7	15.2	80.3	2.7
1979	42.2	15.2	−26.4	10.5
1980	57.7	70.4	−19.0	21.4
1981	−21.3	−26.7	−15.0	−3.4
1982	0.0	6.7	105.9	25.8
1983	25.0	48.6	14.3	24.9
1984	0.0	20.9	8.8	1.6

independence. This will cancel much of the unique risk and still offset part of the market risk.

As an example of how this analysis might be conducted, Table 5–1 shows the return on three stocks and the DJIA for the years 1969–84. These returns were calculated using *Value Line Investment Survey* data for the three stocks and Barron's year-end data for the DJIA. The method is described in Chapter 3, using Table 3–4.

The two oil stocks Exxon and Texaco were selected to demonstrate two issues with common concerns. United Air Lines was picked as a company highly dependent on oil prices as a consumer.

Table 5–2 shows the six correlations for the candidates and the Dow. The computer program in Chapter 10 was used for the computation. The hand method is described in Chapter 3, using Table 3–3 as an example.

The highest correlation is between Texaco and Exxon (63.4681). No surprise here, as both are large companies in the same business. Exxon would have been the best choice over the period studied, but the point is to not have both. United Air Lines moved independently of both Texaco and Exxon and would have made a good portfolio companion for either.

TABLE 5–2 Correlation (R^2)

Company	Texaco	Exxon	United Airlines	Dow Industrials
Texaco	1.0	.634681	.0087411	.446651
Exxon	.634681	1.0	.0581044	.605192
United Airlines	.00874109	.0581044	1.0	.350677
Dow Industrials	.446651	.605	.350677	1.0

All three have some dependence on the Dow Jones Industrial Averages. Sixty percent of the movement in Exxon can be attributed to general market influences. Not too surprising since Exxon is one of the Dow stocks. Texaco is also but went its own way most of the time. United Air Lines was even more independent, being influenced by the market only 35 percent of the time.

None of the stocks or the Dow were inversely related. There are very few stocks that run counter to the market over extended periods, and their selection over other valuation criteria is usually not practical. The decision normally comes down to choosing one of two or three candidates to go with one or two stocks already held. If you don't have access to a computer and can't face the hand calculation, then you might estimate in the following manner:

Plot each pair from the two columns to be correlated in Table 5–1, by the manner used to construct Figure 3–4. If we seek to compare Texaco and Exxon, we might choose to plot Texaco on the horizontal and Exxon on the vertical. The choice is arbitrary as long as you are consistent. The results of the plotting is Figure 5–5.

Note that each of the four areas (quadrants) has been labeled. Count the total points falling in either Quadrant 1 or Quadrant 3. Divide that number by all points plotted and you have an approximation for R^2. If most of the points were in Quadrants 2 and 4, then you would use that number divided by the total, and the relationship would be inverse.

Proper consideration of this principle will be much more effective in managing risk than would doubling the number of stocks in your portfolio.

MAXIM 5–3   Ensure that the correlation is less than 50 percent between any two stocks in your portfolio.

FIGURE 5–5 Texaco versus Exxon

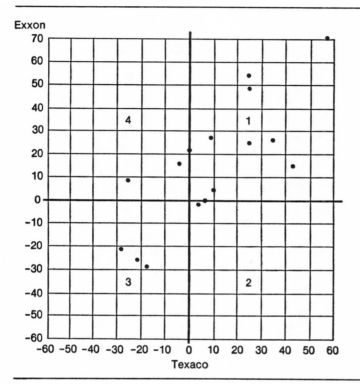

POSITIONING

James B. Rogers turned $2,500 into $14 million in 12 years and then retired. In September 1984 he appeared on Wall Street Week and during the interview made the following comment: "Most of my investments are organic; I start small, and as I build up any kind of confidence and belief, I keep buying *unless the price has gone up.*"

This is the process that I term positioning, and all consistently successful investors do it. They nibble at a stock while their knowledge is increased, their emotions are controlled by downscaled decisions, and time produces an averaging effect on the stocks price.

Risk managed by a diversification of time is as effective as diversifying issues. Also average price is scaled down in a dollar cost–averaging process, making more potential for your holdings.

Starting with the assumption that you're buying troubled companies or buying in a bad market or both, it is most likely that you're buying into a falling market in the stock. My early purchase of a stock invariably is the most expensive. I always buy too soon. Nathan Rothschild claimed to have made his money by buying and selling too soon.

If the stock is rising in price it will soon be out of the extreme undervalued state that I require for buying, and the positioning process is suspended. This has only happened once to me, early in 1975, and I was only able to buy twice before the ebullient market swept prices beyond my buying range.

So whenever you buy, you know there are better prices ahead. The trouble is you don't know just where the bottom will occur, so you put out feelers.

You should only be conducting a buying program in one stock at a time. Liquidating an entire portfolio makes an impossible task of reentry. You shouldn't be buying more than two stocks per year, and you should plan for a six-month accumulation period.

MAXIM 5–4   Liquidate and replace stocks in your portfolio one at a time.

If you have a three-stock portfolio and have just sold one, then you have roughly 35 percent of your capital to be recommitted to a different stock.

You should plan for five purchases over six months, with each purchase involving approximately 7 percent (35/5) of your capital.

The first decision is easy to make, as 7 percent total risk cannot be fatal and the worst scenario will probably only diminish the total portfolio by 2–3 percent.

After a month has passed, more information is available, you have studied the stock's performance, the price is probably better, and failing to detect any fatal fundamental flaw, you buy a second installment.

This process is repeated until you get your 35 percent, the price moves out of range, or you detect insurmountable problems. When problems become more evident, you suspend the buying program and decide whether to stand pat or to liquidate your holdings.

MAXIM 5—5 **Buy each stock in five installments spread over a six-month time period.**

This approach violates another of the market "truisms" of never averaging down. Actually it is more like dollar cost averaging as the price bounces around in the 50 percent undervalued region.

Dollar cost averaging is an approved method of investing consistently small amounts on a regular basis. Because the dollar value is constant, more shares can be bought at lower prices and thereby lower your average cost per share. It's true! For example, if you invest $1,000 at $20 per share and then $1,000 at $10 per share, you'll end up with 150 shares at an average cost of $13.33 per share rather than the $15 you would have averaged had you bought the same number of shares at each price.

The major point is that you spread risk over time. Once you're fully committed you are subject to market conditions and fundamental surprises, but that must be.

The adviser-sanctioned method of entry is to "pyramid" or average up: The problem with this is that it brings the average price up rapidly to where the first reversal may put you at a loss and force an early selling decision. Also if you are averaging up, that means the stock is making a major movement, which may be over before you can get your shares into long-term capital gains status. It's much nicer to be positioned before the move begins, even though this often requires some patience until the action starts.

Another advantage of this patient approach to a position is that you can buy with the limit order: You set an order for the next installment, below the current bid, and let the random walk of the market bring the bargain to you.

Limit Orders

Have you noticed how a stock just purchased closes the day or week at a price lower than you paid even if it eventually works its way significantly higher? Modern portfolio theorists have used their computers to prove that the day-to-day price change in a stock is random and unpredictable. For this reason, it is quite probable that shares may be transacted at more favorable prices than currently quoted, depending on the investor's patience and the volatility of the stock. If there is more than one candidate when purchasing, concurrent bidding allows an even larger discount at the same probability level.

Stocks are normally traded at the market, with your broker getting the best price available at the moment the order reaches the trading floor. You can protect against the imprecision of this process by using the limit order to set the price that you are willing to pay when buying or that you demand when selling. The order can be in effect for a day or indefinitely, with cancellation possible by the investor at any time. As an extreme example of how this can work in the investor's favor, witness this true story:

When the equities markets were in panic in October 1929, trading became entirely unreasonable. Stocks of good companies were dumped at prices representing only a fraction of value.

One of these stocks was White Sewing Machine, a company that had just reported third-quarter earnings of $1.48 and had sold as high as 48 early in 1929.

On Monday, October 28, the stock closed at 11.125. An exchange page, recognizing the lack of reason, entered a limit order for $1 per share. In the frantic trading of October 29, 1929, the order was filled.

The limit order can be prepared logically, without emotion, to take advantage of ragged market action without having to watch the tape continually or deal with the time delay for the order to reach the floor trader's hands. You're always Johnny-on-the-spot if someone wants to sell.

There is no extra fee or commission charged by the broker for entering limit orders. The limit order can be employed to compensate for all commissions, regardless of the frequency of trades. (You buy the stock below the current market in the amount of the commission.) Overall, application of this strategy should improve return on investment by 5 percent for an average holding period of one year. After 30 years, a 5 percent improvement in yield will result in four times as much money for the average investor.

Limit orders specify a price, and there is no guarantee that a transaction will occur. However, the probability of getting a bid at any price level may be computed, and the individual investor may set the limit order in proportion to his desire to own that particular stock. The more candidates that are available, the less important each becomes and the more likely a successful bid at a lower price, as we shall see.

This strategy is modeled on the random tossing of a coin and the resultant accumulation of a surplus of heads or tails over a number of trials. In coin flips, each trial yields a unit gain or loss to the surplus accumulation. Stock going up or down in price are analogous to heads or tails; and if you accept the average daily change in price on a percentage basis as the unit change expected, then coin-flipping statistics would apply and tables of probability can be developed around the number of trails (days) and the excess units desired. Table 5–3 has been developed stochastically on the computer as accumulated unit change for the number of trading days indicated. For example, you have a 50 percent chance of getting a stock at 2.48 units below current price within the next 10 trading days. The unit is the average daily percentage change in the stock being considered.

The unit change can be computed using day-to-day closing price changes in percentage form and averaging these for a reasonable period of time, at least 10 consecutive trading days in length. This should be done just prior to placing the limit order, as volatility is subject to change over time. Table 5–4 demonstrates the computation for a stock, given a beta factor of 1.3 by the *Value Line Investment Survey.* The computation in Table 5–4 suggests that a daily price change averaging 2.086728 percent is a reasonable expectation. This is the unit change, and it differs for each stock and each time period.

Combining the number of units sought and the unit change expected suggests a factor for discounting current price when buying or for a surcharge when selling. Using the 10-day trading period and a 50 percent probability would suggest 2.48 units at 2.086728 percent each, giving a 5.1750854 percent adjustment factor. If our preparation in Table 5–4 is for purchase, then the last (base) price of 12.375 would be discounted by 5.1750854 percent to give a limit price of 11.734584. We would then bid 11.75, with a probability of slightly better than 50 percent of getting the stock in the next 10 trading days. Had we been selling the stock, we would have added a 5.1750854 percent surcharge to the current price, offering it for sale at 13.015416 or 13 even.

In settling on the limit order price, some consideration must be given to "popular" numbers. If your calculation came out to be 20, for example, then you might want to set the order at 20.125

TABLE 5–3 Stock Price Accumulated-Unit Change

Trading Days	Percent of Probability							
	10	20	30	40	50	60	70	80
1	1.15	.95	.83	.73	.66	.60	.54	.46
2	1.98	1.57	1.33	1.13	.98	.87	.74	.59
3	2.80	2.19	1.83	1.53	1.31	1.14	.95	.72
4	3.63	2.80	2.33	1.94	1.63	1.42	1.15	.85
5	4.13	3.18	2.63	2.18	1.83	1.58	1.28	.93
6	4.48	3.47	2.87	2.36	1.97	1.68	1.36	1.00
7	4.81	3.75	3.10	2.54	2.11	1.77	1.43	1.06
8	5.13	4.02	3.32	2.71	2.24	1.86	1.50	1.12
9	5.44	4.28	3.53	2.87	2.36	1.95	1.57	1.18
10	5.73	4.53	3.73	3.03	2.48	2.03	1.63	1.23
11	6.01	4.77	3.92	3.18	2.59	2.11	1.69	1.28
12	6.28	5.00	4.11	3.32	2.70	2.18	1.75	1.33
13	6.54	5.21	4.29	3.46	2.81	2.26	1.81	1.38
14	6.79	5.42	4.46	3.59	2.91	2.33	1.86	1.43
15	7.03	5.62	4.62	3.72	3.01	2.39	1.91	1.47
16	7.25	5.81	4.77	3.84	3.10	2.46	1.96	1.51
17	7.46	5.99	4.92	3.95	3.18	2.52	2.01	1.55
18	7.67	6.17	5.06	4.06	3.27	2.58	2.05	1.59
19	7.86	6.33	5.20	4.16	3.35	2.63	2.10	1.63
20	8.05	6.49	5.33	4.26	3.42	2.68	2.14	1.67
21	8.22	6.63	5.44	4.35	3.49	2.73	2.17	1.70
22	8.38	6.77	5.55	4.44	3.56	2.78	2.21	1.73
23	8.54	6.90	5.66	4.52	3.62	2.82	2.24	1.76
24	8.69	7.02	5.76	4.60	3.68	2.86	2.28	1.78
25	8.83	7.14	5.86	4.68	3.74	2.90	2.30	1.81
26	8.95	7.24	5.94	4.74	3.79	2.93	2.33	1.84
27	9.06	7.34	6.02	4.80	3.83	2.97	2.36	1.86
28	9.17	7.43	6.10	4.86	3.88	3.00	2.38	1.88
29	9.28	7.52	6.17	4.92	3.92	3.03	2.41	1.90
30	9.38	7.61	6.24	4.97	3.96	3.06	2.43	1.91

TABLE 5–4 Computation of Unit Change Percentage

Closing Price	Change	Change Fraction	Change Percentage
$12.75			
12.25	$.50	.50/12.75	3.92156%
12.125	.125	.125/12.25	1.0204
12.25	.125	.125/12.125	1.03092
11.875	.375	.375/12.25	3.06122
12	.125	.125/11.875	1.05263
12.125	.125	.125/12	1.04166
12.5	.375	.375/12.125	3.09278
13.125	.625	.625/12.5	5.0
13	.125	.125/13.125	.95238
13.125	.125	.125/13	.96153
13.25	.125	.125/13.125	.95238
14.125	.875	.875/13.25	6.60377
13.75	.375	.375/14.125	2.65486
13.25	.5	.5/13.75	3.63636
13.25	.0	.0/13.25	0.0
12.875	.375	.375/13.25	2.83018
12.875	.0	.0/12.875	0.0
12.625	.25	.25/12.875	1.94174
12.625	.0	.0/12.625	0.0
12.375	.25	.25/12.625	1.98019
Total			41.73456

NOTE: Twenty changes totaling 41.73456 will average 2.086728 percent per day for the period.

when buying and 19.875 when selling, in order to avoid the lines that form at round numbers.

A bidding strategy is most useful to the investor who has more than one candidate for purchase and the patience to wait up to 30 trading days to complete a transaction. If you have more than one candidate, then you can bid concurrently and lower the probability of each. Two bids with 50 percent probability on each will result in at least one purchase 75 percent of the time. Three would yield an 87.5 percent expectation of success. Stated another way, each of three probabilities could be lowered to 40 percent and have a 78.4 percent combinatorial probability of getting at least one. Table 5–5 demonstrates the probability of at least one success, where all candidates have the same individual probability. In actual practice you may want a different level of probability on each candidate, based on your priorities for ownership. Thus a most desirable stock might be given a 50 percent probability bid, while two less attractive ones might have 40 and 30 percent probabilities.

TABLE 5–5 Probability of at Least One Successful Bid for Multiple Limit Orders

Individual Probability	Number of Stocks				
	One	Two	Three	Four	Five
10	10	19	27	34	41
20	20	36	49	59	67
30	30	51	66	76	83
40	40	64	78	87	92
50	50	75	88	94	97
60	60	84	94	97	99
70	70	91	97	99	100
80	80	96	99	100	100
90	90	99	100	100	100

The combination probability can be computed by calculating the probability of failure and then subtracting from 100. If the probabilities of getting three stocks are 50, 40, and 30 percent, then the probabilities of not getting each are 50/100, 60/100, and 70/100, respectively. In theoretical statistics, the probability of multiple events is the product of individual probabilities. In our example this would be a failure probability of $50 \times 60 \times 70/100 \times 100 \times 100$ or 210,000/1,000,000, which is 21 percent. If this is the probability of total failure, then the probability of at least one success is $100 - 21$, or 79 percent.

As mentioned earlier, there is no guarantee that a transaction will occur; and when more than one bid has been made, it is possible that all bids will be executed. If you have the resources to back the transactions, then multiple purchases accelerate the positioning process, and if the market weakness is temporary, it may turn out to be opportunity at its best. However, if the buying exceeds your resources, then you must reverse the excessive transactions at the expense of commissions. If the market is normal while your limit orders are in effect, then the broker can be instructed to cancel all additional orders after the first one fills.

If you bid on two stocks, each with a 40 percent chance of success, then both will be filled 16 percent of the time $(40 \times 40)/(100 \times 100)$. This assumes the orders to be active for the entire period planned or that a market break carries both to your bid levels concurrently.

You may want to instruct your broker carefully on cancellation policy. Brokers don't like limit orders and will try to discourage you. It represents more effort on their part and the possibility of no commission. Limit orders may be used on all stocks except a very few low-priced issues (usually below $3). Odd lots may be filled at one tick (eighth) below a buy order or above a sell order to compensate the odd-lot broker. If the broker says that he can't place a limit order for any normally priced stock, then change brokers!

At least three stocks to bid on, a 30-day waiting period, and average volatility in each stock should on balance result in 4.9 percent savings 80 percent of the time. When the stock is sold, the multiple strategy is not likely, so that 1.9 percent at 80 percent probability will bring the overall result to 6.8 percent. If the average holding period is 1 year and the investment continues to compound, after 25 years there will be five times as much money, regardless of the return through the years. If volatility is greater than average, then the impact is even more dramatic.

When to Sell

"A time to get, and a time to lose: a time to keep and a time to cast away." Ecclesiastes 3:6 applies very well to the stock market. It's difficult to make a mistake in buying stock, if we know when to sell.

Unfortunately, when to sell is one of those things that neither our mothers nor our brokers have told us. Everybody has some advice on when and what to buy but rarely tells you how to escape from the earlier advice.

It is most difficult and something you have to do on your own. Half the time it means admitting a mistake, which is hard on our egos—especially traumatic if we've shared a "sure thing" with others and are now subject to a public confessional.

Let's dissect the problem and see if we can apply some mechanical rules that simplify the decision process:

1. The losses should be easily handled, but they usually cause the majority of unduly delayed decisions. Use the short-term tax law and purge all losers prior to the stock becoming a long-term capital loss. You've heard this before and you'll hear it again, but you must keep losses short term. There will be some tax advantage for everyone; but most important, it stops a bleeding of both time and capital.

2. The second case is that of the clear-cut winner. Again, use the tax law and allow this stock to go long term. Once it reaches that status, the analysis becomes more difficult, although pleasant.

Just because the stock is now eligible for long-term capital gains treatment does not necessarily require a sale—it may be a time to enjoy. Even if the stock seems fully valued, recognize that the market will carry it to an overvalued state once "the crowd" gets the urge.

The principal measure of enthusiasm is volume of transactions. As a rule-of-thumb, once a stock is "discovered" there are about six months of increased volume and rising prices before the crowd loses interest. The volume tends to peak about halfway through the rise.

As long as interest continues and the stock performs relatively well compared to the general market, leave it alone. Let it cook!

Conversely, if the stock starts to sputter, sell it and walk away—never looking back. I like to sell with a limit order above the market—but not too far above, as it's basically a buyer's market and you're now a seller. I never use a stop order, as you're guaranteeing a price below some previously attained level and consequently giving back some of your gain. I'm not inflexible about the limit order on selling and will sell at the market if the stock is behaving erratically.

If you can't decide if the stock is still performing you may want to sell part of your holdings. Occasionally I'll sell half or take out my original investment when I'm uncertain about what to do. You also have to consider if you have a place to put money raised by the sale.

3. The third case is the most difficult. The stock approaches long-term status with neither clear-cut loss nor gain. You should review the fundamentals, and if everything is in place, then patience is in order. Dividends help keep the faith. If the stock is still dead after two years, bury it!

The first six months of involvement with a stock are for accumulation. The next six months are for observation. If the stock does well, the third six-month period is spent seeking the right time to sell. This is the model, but be prepared for real-life variations.

CHAPTER 6

Money Management

A fool and his money are soon parted.
—*James Howell*

In the past my children would come to me for a dollar (now it's a hundred times that), and I'd give them a minilecture: "This isn't a dollar you're asking for. It's really $11.81 if you compound it quarterly at 10 percent for 25 years." I would hardly get warmed up to the subject when they'd interrupt with, "Never mind, we'll go ask Mom!" That was fine with me because I got to keep my $11.81 ($1 present value) and I knew their mother's dollar was gone, whether she spent it or they did!

My dad often said: "It's not what you earn, it's what you save." Lots of truth in that, but I would extend it one step farther and say that it's also how you manage what you save.

Remember the biblical parable of the talents in Matthew 25:14–30:

> For the kingdom of heaven is as a man traveling in a far country, who called his servants, and delivered unto them his goods.
>
> And unto one he gave five talents, to another two, and to another one; to every man according to his several abilities; and straightway took his journey.
>
> Then he that had received the five talents went and traded with the same, and made them other five talents.
>
> And likewise he that had received two, he also gained other two.
>
> But he that had received one went and digged in the earth, and hid his lord's money.
>
> After a long time the lord of those servants cometh, and reckoneth with them.
>
> And so he that had received five talents came and brought other five talents, saying, Lord, thou deliveredst unto me five talents: behold, I have gained beside them five talents more.

His lord said unto him: Well done, thou good and faithful servant: thou hast been faithful over a few things, I will make thee ruler over many things: enter thou into the joy of thy lord.

He also that had received two talents came and said, Lord, thou deliveredst unto me two talents: behold, I have gained two other talents beside them.

His lord said unto him: Well done, good and faithful servant; thou hast been faithful over a few things, I will make thee ruler over many things: enter thou into the joy of thy lord.

Then he which had received the one talent came and said, Lord, I knew thee that thou art a hard man, reaping where thou hast not sown, and gathering where thou hast not strewed:

And I was afraid, and went and hid thy talent in the earth: lo, there thou hast that is thine.

His lord answered and said unto him, Thou wicked and slothful servant, thou knewest that I reap where I sowed not, and gather where I have not strewed:

Thou oughtest therefore to have put my money to the exchangers, and then at my coming I should have received my own with usury.

Take therefore the talent from him, and give it unto him that hath 10 talents.

For unto everyone that hath shall be given, and he shall have abundance: but from him that hath not shall be taken away even that which he hath.

And cast ye the unprofitable servant into outer darkness: there shall be weeping and gnashing of teeth."

The point of the parable is that money is employable and that it is sinful for it to lie idle and be ravished by time. (Yes, I know the broader moral of getting the most out of our ability.)

Time can be an ally, or it can be the enemy. If you owe money, time can be devastating. Look at the total interest paid on your house over a 20- to 30-year amortization schedule. A $50,000 mortgage at 14 percent paid monthly over 25 years costs $130,564 in total interest. (model in Chapter 10). Of course inflation moderates that somewhat, as you're paying off with deflated dollars downstream. Still, if you reverse the process to become the payee rather than the payer, then time becomes your employee. Remember Rockefeller and his potato money.

Most of us are catching on to using other people's money, and some of us have incorporated the principle of "float" to extend the benefits. I put everything I can on credit cards and then time my payment each month to reach the bank on the last day prior to an interest charge. I pay the balance with a check on an out-of-state bank, which extends the use another 2–4 days. This amounts to free use of nearly $2,000. Invested at 10 percent for 25 years this becomes $23,620 (remember my lecture, kids!).

My general guidelines for managing money are:

1. Don't spend it until you absolutely have to.
2. Keep it employed at all times.
3. Know just what rate of return you're receiving.
4. When you must spend it, pay cash only if you can't invest for more than the use rate that will be charged you.
5. Know your tax bracket and look for any tax advantage.

Let's break the science of managing money into component parts and examine each in turn.

COMPOUND INTEREST

Einstein was fascinated by the effect of compound interest, and Baron de Rothschild called it the eighth wonder of the world. Men like Franklin and Carnegie employed it to the perpetual good of society through foundations.

Benjamin Franklin left 1,000 pounds each to Boston and Philadelphia. In today's dollars that would be about $60,000 for each city. The Bostonians built Franklin Union, and Philadelphia created the Franklin Institute. Both funds are still well endowed, with Boston's exceeding $3 million. Carnegie's gift has more than doubled, while distributing over 200 percent of what he contributed. It apparently can't be spent nearly as quickly as it multiplies.

Some people have ensured the continuation of their fortune by skipping one or more generations and letting the money compound for future progeny. A $1 million investment in 30-year bonds held in trust for a grandchild at current rates of 12 percent would be worth $33 million in the year 2015.

We consider the American Indians to have been fleeced by Peter Minuit in 1626 when they gave up their right to Manhattan Island for $24 worth of wampum. Incidentally, wampum (beads or shells) was the official currency in that day.

Had the Indians been able to put their $24 in one of the perpetual government bonds being issued in Holland around that time at, say, 8 percent and continued reinvesting at the same rate, today the government would have paid out $40,749,700,000,000. The Indians could not only have exacted their revenge by bankrupting Holland, they then could have repurchased Manhattan Island with all it's assets—lock, stock, and computer.

The effect of compound interest is more evident in zero-coupon bonds. For less than 10 cents on the dollar, you can buy a zero-coupon bond that will pay the dollar in 20 years for a compounded yield of 12 percent. The only problem is that Uncle Sam wants his tax dollars along the way, even though you get nothing until the bond matures in 20 years.

There are three variables involved in the compounding process: time, rate, and frequency of compounding. Time and rate are equally significant in terms of percentage increases in your capital. The frequency of compounding has a very minor effect on the end result. Compounding once or twice a year retains the essence of the process, even though daily compounding will produce a slightly better return. Given a choice, a quarter-point better rate will overcome more frequent compounding.

Think in terms of future value and let the magic of compound interest perform for you.

TAXES

Ben Franklin said that the only things certain were death and taxes. Don't tell me you're not a large enough investor to be concerned with taxes. My answer to that is that you must be cognizant of your taxes or you'll never be a large investor.

Most people don't become concerned with taxes until the April 15 deadline approaches. After computing the bite that is to be donated to the government, we resolve to do something about it next year but rarely do.

The time to do your tax work is in the fall of the taxable year, when the full year's result is visible but enough time remains to manage the taxes. In October 1986 start your tax work for 1986.

The records will be incomplete, but income levels should be predictable and a rough computation can be accomplished. Then go one step farther and work an estimate for 1987. The data will be sparse, but at least an estimate of above- or below-average tax burden should emerge.

Consider any possible tax laws that might be enacted in the next tax year that could take away (or improve) deductions and the effect this will work on the total tax debt for the two years.

Let's look at some general guidelines first, and then we'll get to individual tax-saving ideas:

First of all, you shouldn't avoid taking a profit just because there is a significant tax to be paid. This pertains to investments that have long-term capital gains treatment, and the only way remaining to reduce expected taxes is for value to decrease or the investor's tax bracket to be reduced drastically. If you think it will no longer pay its way, do what you can to mitigate the taxes and then sell the investment.

Now I'll suggest something that seems to conflict with the above: that is, to delay taxes. This can be done in several ways. The individual retirement account (IRA) is a prime example. Others are reinvested electric utility dividends, tax-deferred annuities, short sale of stock against the box, and partially tax-deferred utility dividends. We'll discuss each in turn.

Any time that the tax payment can be delayed means that you now have an interest-free government loan and that you can choose the most favorable tax rate in your future for paying it off.

The alert investor has some ability to blunt extreme years by managing expenses, gifts, and other deductions and by income averaging when appropriate.

There are other methods of avoiding or reducing taxes through capital gains and losses, municipal securities, and trusts. The principal strategy should be:

1. Convert ordinary income to capital gains whenever possible.
2. Take long-term capital gains and short-term capital losses.
3. Record losses and gains in separate years, with losses first if possible.
4. Delay payment.
5. Take expenses and make contributions in years of high earnings.

The tax code defines loss or gain on property held for investment (such as stocks, bonds, or land and property held for business) and personal use (such as houses, equipment, etc.) to be capital loss or gain. Items meeting the definition are given better tax treatment than ordinary income. If these assets have produced a gain and have been held long term (currently six months and one day), then only 40 percent of the profit is subject to tax as ordinary income. Conversely, any loss that is recorded in short term (six months or less) will reduce ordinary income dollar for dollar. If the loss is long term, then only 50 percent of the loss may be used in reducing ordinary income.

Multiple investments must be combined to produce net gains or losses, and the combinations usually will wash out some of the advantage to the investor. By his choice of when to sell the property, the investor has some control over optimizing the tax situation.

Income produced by the property is usually considered to be ordinary income, with each additional dollar being taxed at the investor's tax bracket. People in the 35 percent bracket would give 35 cents of each additional investment-produced ordinary income dollar to Uncle Sam.

To encourage investment the Congress has enacted laws allowing some change of status for ordinary income. Municipal bonds issued by state and local governments yield income free of federal taxation. The rate of return is lower than comparable fully taxed investments, which is an advantage to the issuing authority. The federal government benefits by the reduction of revenue sharing with the states. Once thought to be the province of the rich, municipal bonds with current yield near 10 percent may be attractive to investors near the 25 percent bracket, if taxable rates are 12 percent (12 percent reduced by 25 percent tax is 9 percent net).

Any kind of retirement plan that allows funding with tax-deductible contributions allows the tax to be deferred. Most notable of these is the individual retirement account. You can contribute up to $2,000 per working individual and deduct the entire amount when you file your tax return. If you're in the 35 percent tax bracket, this means an actual tax reduction of $700. Just that $700 alone, if placed in a sinking fund each year at 12 percent, would be worth $50,436.60 after 20 years. This is found money, as Uncle Sam would have taken it and *overspent* it. You must have an IRA, even if you have to borrow money to fund it. The type of investment is your choice, but zero-coupon bonds are attractive at times of high interest rates, as you can lock up high yields for long term with relatively small principal.

The point is that the IRA (or the Keogh plan, if qualified) is too good to pass up. It is eventually taxed as ordinary income, but you have delayed payment, have use of the money, and have some choice of tax rate when you do pay the taxes. Just be sure you don't use some tax-protected investment such as municipal bonds in your IRA and thereby lose a second tax advantage.

Tax-deferred annuities operate on the same principle, with just your money being involved in deferring ordinary income until maturity of the annuity. However you lose the right to manage the money. Trusts don't defer tax payments but lower them to the bracket of the relative that the money is entrusted to. The problem is that you lose control and management of the money— at least temporarily.

The Economic Recovery Tax Act of 1981 allows certain electric utility company dividends to be tax deferred if reinvested. The limits are $750 per individual or $1,500 per couple. The act is scheduled to expire at the end of 1985 unless there is pressure to extend it. When the stock purchased from the dividends is sold, the amount received is treated as a capital gain with a cost basis of zero. Again, you choose when to sell and thereby choose your tax bracket. Even if the tax advantage is eliminated, you have the continuing advantages of dollar cost averaging, no commissions, possibly discounted pricing (some companies discount 3 to 5 percent), and disciplined investment.

Utility companies often pay part of their dividends out of their capital when profits don't cover the dividend for the year. You then adjust the cost of your shares by the amount determined to be return of capital and do not declare that amount as ordinary income. Eventually the deferred amount is treated as capital gain— that is, the acquiring cost is reduced when the stock is sold. Ordinary income is now capital gains, with 60 percent excluded from taxation, your choice of tax bracket, and interim use of the tax money.

The negatives are:

1. The company has income problems and may have subpar growth during the time you own the stock.
2. The status of future dividends is unpredictable.

A strategy that I've used for several years is to consult the broker's list of companies with a history of return of capital and to choose several in order to get some tax deferral each year. When a company gets back on the profit track, you take your capital gain and replace it with another troubled utility.

In 1984 I sold Dominion Resources, which I began accumulating as Virginia Electric in 1975. There was tax-deferred income in 1976, 1979, 1980, 1981, and 1982 totaling $8,728.91. I purchased stock over an eight-year period for a total of $46,095.93. I received a net of $70,283.28 from the sale. Reduction of cost by $8,728.91 gave an adjusted cost of $37,367.02 and a long-term capital gain of $32,916.26. I received $24,857.50 in dividends, with 35 percent tax deferred. I chose a year to sell when my tax bracket would be low and was taxed approximately \$628 on the return of capital.

As speculators, we are primarily concerned with the appreciation of capital by increased pricing of the property. The fundamental rule is long-term gains and short-term losses. I've said this a lot, but it cannot be overemphasized. Philosophically, when you look at your record you'll find that your gains should have been held longer (rarely do we get it all) and your losses should have been sold sooner (never should have been bought, actually!). The next best thing is to use the tax law to decide the issue.

MAXIM 6–1   Sell losses short term; hold gains long term.

Ideally the loss should occur in this year, and the gain should be passed until next year. Separation maximizes the advantages of each (see example in Chapter 1). By establishing the loss first, you get back some tax money to use immediately and delay tax on gains for another year.

Establishing the loss is easy, but how do we postpone the gain without seeing the market ravage the price in the interim? By selling short against the box! The box is your lockbox (or the broker's) and the certificates that exist there.

By selling short you establish a price but delay the delivery of certificates until later (after the first of the new year). When the certificates are delivered, the transaction is completed, and that is the record date for tax purposes. Be sure the stock is in long-term status before executing the short sale, as that date (not delivery) determines capital gains status. The general rule of thumb is to accelerate loss sales and delay gains.

MAXIM 6–2   Sell losses this year, gains next year.

In years of exceptional gain, income averaging can be useful. The rule is that your averageable income must exceed 140 percent of the average of the prior three years.

Don't forget margin interest as a deductible. You're limited to \$10,000 plus net investment income. In years of exceptional income, you should accelerate any investment expenses that you anticipate having (seminars, books, etc.), as a larger share will be paid by Uncle Sam.

TABLE 6–1 Tax Examples for Joint Returns

	Alpha	Beta
Earned income	$30,000	$30,000
Long-term capital gains	20,000	0
Short-term capital gains	0	20,000
Taxable interest	0	10,000
Deferred dividends	10,000	0
Dividend exclusion	200	0
Individual retirement account	4,000	0
Excess deductions	5,000	5,000
Exemptions	5,200	5,200
Taxable income	23,600	49,800
Tax	3,166	10,981

Table 6–1 shows the tax extremes for two people of relatively similar circumstances. Mr. Alpha has done what he can to avoid (not evade) taxes. Mr. Beta has ignored the whole problem. The bottom line reflects $7,815.40 difference in their tax bills. Put that amount in a sinking fund, let it compound year after year at 12 percent, and you can retire comfortably in less than 20 years. Work it out!

Taxes are a very complex topic and subject to constant change. You need to consult a tax expert or educate yourself on the details. I only wanted to introduce some ideas and alert you to the impact that taxes will have on the retention of capital. It's not enough to make it—you have to find a way to keep it.

COMMISSIONS

"The broker made money, the firm made money, and two out of three ain't bad!" This anonymous, tongue-in-cheek quote has a message for us. So does the old story told about a prospective investor being taken to the yacht club for lunch, and his broker points out ownership of the vessels. "This one belongs to Broker Smith, and this one to Broker Jones." Whereupon the prospective client interrupts the broker with the moot question, "Where are the customers' yachts?"

Though I consider myself an investor rather than a trader, averaging nearly 14 months for each holding and less than a 4 percent commission rate, still I have paid nearly $50,000 in commissions during my investment career. Consider what this might have meant had I been able to retain and invest that amount!

Of course the commission rate is low compared to taxes, passing of dividends, or margin interest. It is a necessary part of doing business and must be managed as you would any other business expense. It is deductible, as you're only taxed on net profit.

How do we manage the commission? You can trade stocks without commission if you can find the buyer/seller that is willing to deal directly with you. If you're not particular in what you're acquiring and are willing to accept the number of shares offered, then trades can be arranged for just the cost of a transfer fee. I've bought a friend's stock by agreeing to the closing price on a certain day, having the certificates endorsed to me and taken to the bank to initiate a transfer. No commission, but not practical.

Many companies have a plan where you can reinvest dividends, plus add limited additional capital to buy shares without commission. Some even discount their shares 3 to 5 percent when bought with dividends.

New issues of stocks and bonds are paid by the underwriting process, without additional commission, until trade begins. I recently had a bond called away from me without commission.

But these are special circumstances, and to get the shares we want when we want them, we must deal with someone qualified to buy and sell that stock.

In recent years the emergence of the discount broker has provided a viable option for the small investor to significantly reduce his commission expense.

I still use a full-service brokerage firm because of my entangled finances and the efficiency of my broker and because my trades are large enough to be discounted. If I were starting over, were to move, or lost the broker, then I'd work with one or more discounters.

When people like me have passed out of the system, the full-service firm must cut fees to compete. There will always be a certain number of people that want to have their hands held by a broker, but the big business is moving toward the discount house.

Table 6–2 demonstrates some fee differences between full-service and discount brokerage firms. Most firms structure their fees around the total dollar amount, number of shares, and price of each share. Commissions on low-priced shares will vary widely at different brokerage firms. It does pay to shop around.

TABLE 6–2 Sample Commissions

		Full-Service		Discount	
Shares	Price	Fee	Percent	Fee	Percent
100	$ 5	$ 40	8 %	$ 34	6.8 %
100	10	40	4	35	3.5
100	50	99	1.98	74	.98
500	5	116.50	4.66	59	2.36
500	10	149	2.98	74	1.48
500	50	384	1.54	134	.54

All firms offer margin, research, and good execution. Advice is only offered at the full-service firm, but most of us would be better off without that service.

It would probably pay to check with three or four brokerage firms before starting any buying program. If you're planning to use margin, check that rate also and compute the expenses for the expected holding period. You may have to pay a bigger commission but could get it back on interest rates.

Keep the effect of commissions in proportion. Don't avoid the need to buy or sell, but limit the tendency to trade and, given a choice, try to buy higher-priced stock in larger blocks. Installment buying will create more commissions, but stock can be sold in a complete block and thereby the commission percentage reduced.

DIVIDENDS

Shortly after Andrew Carnegie bought his 10 shares of Adams Express stock, an envelope appeared on his desk, addressed to Andrew Carnegie, Esquire. Inside was a check for $10, representing his first dividend on the stock. Andrew exclaimed in delight: "Eureka, here is the goose that lays the golden egg!"

This represented the first money that Carnegie had received that hadn't been earned by the sweat of his brow, and if anyone ever knew a good thing when he saw it, it was Andrew Carnegie.

Yet we are often told to ignore the dividend yield when selecting stocks. Better still, we're advised to seek stocks that don't have a dividend, as they can be expected to grow faster and capital gain is preferable to dividend income.

I agree that capitals gains are preferable, but there is no evidence of an inverse relationship between dividend yield and price appreciation. In fact the informal studies I've conducted show no relationship whatever. Given a choice, the investor should always take the higher yield.

I've mentioned earlier that the dividend can cancel out both commissions and inflation and that it calms your emotions when you're receiving some return from a lagging stock. What we haven't considered is that a high-yielding stock, when the dividend is secure or increasing, sometimes will attract enough buyers to create a significant capital gain just because of the attractive yield.

Utility stocks that I have bought for income in the early 1980s (and bonds too, for that matter) have virtually all doubled as more and more investors became attracted to the generous yield. The best-performing funds of 1984 were utility-based income funds, while the poorest performers were high-tech growth funds. An exceptional year, obviously, but historically the Dow has grown 4 percent per year in price and 5 percent via dividend. It's nice to have something compounding on a scheduled basis while you're waiting for the ups and downs of the market to resolve.

To illustrate the power of dividends and compounding while avoiding commissions and taxes, let me use another personal example: When the Economic Recovery Act of 1981 allowed reinvested dividends to be designated as tax deferred, I bought 1,000 shares of Utah Power and Light to be the investment vehicle for this tax break. The market price at the end of 1981 was 17⅞, and the dividend was $2.28 per share (12.75 percent yield).

Utah Power and Light was chosen as a stock that was not likely to have any return of capital tax-deferred yield, so I wouldn't negate an advantage by reinvesting the dividends in additional shares. The $2,280 in dividends each year more than covers the $1,500 that can be deferred.

Each quarter, the company purchases as many shares as my quarterly dividend allows, based on the market price at closing on the last day of the quarter. These shares in turn earn a dividend the following quarter, and a compounding process occurs four times a·year.

At the original yield (12.75 percent) the investment should double in less than six years ($72 \div 12.75 = 5.65$). However, two other factors are accelerating the process. The share prices have risen, and the dividend has been increased slightly.

After 3½ years there are 1,442 shares at a market value of $36,050. That's a 44.2 percent increase in shares and a 101 percent increase in capital.

I have had to pay taxes on dividends beyond $1,500 each year. The original annual dividend of $2,280 will have grown to over $3,500 by the end of 1985, mostly due to additional shares.

This gives you some idea of how fast dollars can breed, given the right environment. Of course, much of the dollar gain is due to a 40 percent increase in share price. However, this has had a negative effect on the total number of shares, as prices have been more expensive each quarter and so fewer shares can be bought. The ideal arrangement would have been for the stock to go down for effective dollar cost averaging and then increase in price prior to sale.

MAXIM 6–3   Seek enough dividend yield to cover commissions and inflation.

MARGIN

Shakespeare counseled us to "neither a lender nor a borrower be," but then Shakespeare didn't have an opportunity to play the stock market!

Jesse Livermore had the following thought about buying stock on margin (borrowed money): "What use is there in being right unless you get all the good possible out of it?"

Margin is a dirty word among investors. We never hesitate to buy a car with 20 percent down but frown on stocks being bought with 50 percent down. The car is a depreciating luxury that will be made more expensive by the use of borrowed money, while the investment is good business.

Apparently the poor connotation afforded margin goes back to the abuses of the 1920s, when stocks were bought for 10 cents equity on the dollar. Margin use has been blamed for the crash, even though there were only 1 million margin accounts at the time. The same low down payment can be made today against commodities and index futures, with no apparent worries about damage to the financial structure.

The tendency is to focus on the negative aspect of margin use, particularly the threat to your capital. The broker will prevent you from destroying more than your original investment, since the law requires him to demand more equity or sell enough of your position to satisfy the margin maintenance requirement.

So you could lose your entire investment. But you could do that on your own, without any help from margin. That's a risk you must be willing to take in order to reap the rewards of speculating in stocks.

Where the concern should be directed, but rarely is, is to interest that must be paid on the borrowed money. If your investment doesn't return enough after taxes and commissions to offset the net interest charges after taxes, then you shouldn't be borrowing. You probably shouldn't be investing in stocks at all in this situation.

However, if you have an established record of return that exceeds the average expected cost of money for the period anticipated for ownership of the stock, then it makes sense to amplify that net return as much as possible.

Assume for a moment that you can reach the 25 percent average rate of return. Fully margined, the rate doubles to 50 percent. Pay your interest charges, and you net 40 percent before taxes. After 20 years you have more than 10 times as much money than you would have without margin, regardless of your starting fund.

My rates are 26 percent, after commissions, prior to taxes. By using margin most of the time but rarely using all that is available to me, I have managed to increase my fund by 36 percent average after taxes. Margin has had a very positive effect for me, with only the late 1974 period threatening my principal. In that case I chose to support my position (more borrowed money), and it paid off handsomely. Compare 1975 to 1974 in Figure 1−5.

Since the law was enacted in 1934 the Federal Reserve has the right to set the requirements for the investor's equity as a percentage of the market value of the securities. This has ranged from 40 percent to 100 percent but has remained at 50 percent for stocks in recent years. The investor must put up at least $1 for a $2 investment.

Should the investment fall in market value, the investor must keep his equity above the maintenance level, which is 25 percent by law but 30−35 percent as required by brokerage firms.

A stock bought with full margin would trigger a margin maintenance call at most brokerage firms when market value dropped by 25 percent. (Your equity drops twice as fast as the market, not considering interest charges.)

Since I expect 25 percent losses one fourth of the time, why haven't I had more margin calls? Mainly because I always have two or more stocks, with a winner usually offsetting my loser. 1974 was an unusually bad time for all stocks, and I kept loading up in anticipation of the bottom. You can compute and anticipate a margin call by the following method: Equity is market value of the portfolio, less all debt. Equity divided by market value must be .35 or greater (.30 at some firms). If you divide the equity by .35, you get the market value level below which additional funds will be requested. If trading is closed for the day with your market value below that level, then a margin call will be automatically issued.

The problem can be complicated by the type of security. Some over-the-counter issues cannot be borrowed on and are considered part of a cash account. Those priced below $10 may require a minimum $5 equity level. Corporate bonds require only 30 percent down and federal securities 8 percent. The borrowing power (money available for additional purchases) is something that I've never been able to calculate accurately on my own account. It is part of my monthly statement but remains a mystery as to its computation.

To summarize, the advantages of margin use are:

1. It provides leverage to improve profits when a good opportunity occurs.
2. The rate of interest is reasonable—usually better than otherwise available.
3. The interest charges are tax deductible.

INFLATION

Rip Van Winkle woke up in the year 2000 and rushed to the telephone to call his broker: "Hey, this is Rip, and I've been asleep for 20 years. How are my stocks doing?" The broker dug through his files and told Rip that his portfolio was now worth $1.5 million. Before Rip could express his pleasure, the operator broke into the conversation with: "Please deposit $100,000 for the next three minutes!"

Not likely to happen, you say! You're right, but probably for the wrong reason. If we have hyperinflation, the stock market won't benefit. The market likes a little inflation (no deflation, thank you!), but exceptional inflation means higher interest rates and money leaving stocks and bonds.

Historically we have had two periods of extreme, sustained inflation. The first began about 1520 and lasted 100 years, fueled by gold and silver taken to Europe from the Americas. The second period began at the end of the World War II. Other than these two periods, we have enjoyed relative price stability for hundreds of years, with any price surges being quickly corrected. Using 15th-century prices as a base of 100, the 16th-century precious-metals discoveries raised the price index to the neighborhood of 600. The next 200 years saw the index fluctuate between 400 and 600. The Napoleonic wars raised it near 1,000, only to see it retreat again to the 600 level just before World War II. Since that time there has been a steady progression to over 7000 on this index. The consumer price index has just about doubled since 1975 for an average inflation rate of over 7 percent ($72 \div 10 = 7.2$).

That means your buying power has been cut in half during that time. A $5,000 car in 1975 costs $10,000 today. The stock indexes haven't preserved your buying power. The Dow Jones Industrial Averages closed 1975 at 852.41 and would need to reach 1700 to have kept pace. Of course there were dividends, and an average 5 percent added to the 4 percent growth in the Dow would have given a real rate of return near 2 percent.

Thus it is a real battle just to preserve your buying power, let alone improve it significantly. In terms of constant dollars, the DJIA peaked at the end of 1965 and today is worth only one third of that in 1965 dollars. The low inflation period of 1953–65 saw the buying power of the index triple in constant dollars.

What is the message here? In times of relatively low inflation, equities are definitely the place to be. During periods of accelerating inflation, the money should be moved to hard assets (gold, real estate, etc.).

There is a very high positive correlation between the percentage change in the consumer price index and the percentage change in the price of gold. There is pretty much the same relationship between inflation (percentage change in the consumer price index) and interest rates. If you think inflation is increasing, then expect rising gold prices and falling bond prices.

The bond market is particularly difficult to predict, especially in periods of relatively low inflation. Today inflation is approximately 4 percent, with many claiming that we are really in a deflationary environment. The bond market is skeptical, as long-term bonds yield near 12 percent, implying 6 percent *expected* inflation. If we have a return to the 7 percent average of recent years, the bond market would be a disaster.

The stock market is not so risky. It is a market of stocks, and there are always a number that will do their own thing regardless of the economy. But rising inflation and, hence, interest rates eventually induce recession with reduced earnings and reduced stock prices.

No easy solutions—just a caution to keep a weather eye on inflation and adjust your portfolio accordingly.

CHAPTER 7

Losing Games

Men are apt to believe what they least understand.
—*Montaigne*

Twenty years ago the average investor could choose from savings bonds, a savings account (bank or savings and loan), real estate, or stocks. The choices were straightforward and the risks visible.

Today the investor faces hundreds of complicated investments with a myriad of overlaid strategies. It is impossible for them to be fully understood by the broker of investments, let alone an average investor. The broker has yelled uncle, asking for relief from new "products"; but the investor, lamb that he is, eagerly awaits each new fleecing. When stock options lost some of their glamour, index futures were created. Now we have options on index futures, and the casino expands.

Recently I heard a commodities broker, advertising on the Financial News Network, compare his fees to full-service brokerage firms in the following manner: "The truth is that the average commodities trader making one round-trip trade per week will be broke in one year. At my firm the commissions are so low that at the end of the year you'll still have 80 percent of your money to work with. How's that for a difference?" From all indications he is doing a booming business. Are people that stupid, or do they want to lose, or is it that they just like the game?

Most of the games being concocted now are exciting. They offer exceptional leverage and produce violent swings in fortune. Imaginative new systems use Fibonacci numbers, Kondratieff waves, sunspots, and superbowl indicators. Many of the investors don't know if they want their market to go up or down, but they keep stepping up to the table. It's not whether you win or lose, it's how you play the game!

Well, to me it's whether I win or lose, and I play the game accordingly. Admittedly I play a dull game, often inactive for months at a time, but I do win. I don't consider myself a gambler. I can spend days in Reno or Las Vegas, enjoying the entertainment, and never place a bet. It bothers me to lose a dollar at a sports bet, but I can take thousands of dollars of stock loss without exceptional distress. That's business and part of the expectation.

Thoreau gave good advice over 100 years ago when he said, "Simplify." If you don't understand something, you should study it. If you still don't understand, then simplify the process. If that isn't possible, then avoid the entire issue. It's a sure bet that anything too complicated to understand fully is going to end up costing you money—even more so if you've been promised extravagant or unreal return on your money. The only sure principle in investing is that expected return is in direct proportion to the total risk.

So let's examine some of the games and see if I can present the logic of why they should be avoided.

SHORT SELLING

The market goes down as well as up. Why shouldn't we take advantage of declines by reversing the buy-sell process? It shouldn't be an ethics problem, as playing the stocks both ways lends additional stability to the market? There are periods of decline where the market indexes will lose 25 percent or more. Does it make sense to just step aside during this time? I've been a short-seller in the past and more successful than I had a right to be—but never again, because of the reasons I now want to lay before you.

First of all, you are opposing a trend. In the past the markets have grown at about 4 percent per year. That is about the rate of inflation averaged over any consistent period of time. The markets are stable or inclining almost two thirds of the time and only in decline one third of the time. What makes you think you can overcome 2–1 odds in predicting market direction to be down?

OK, so I've been telling you to ignore market direction and deal with individual stocks. Your short candidate is so overvalued that it has to fall, regardless of market direction. So let's talk timing.

In 1968, I sold Control Data short at 117⅞. If ever there was an overvalued stock, that was it. Two months later I shorted again at 106¾, and then the stock went up. The market was good, but

Control Data was better. To compound the problem, it was on the active list day after day, and every time I turned on the radio, someone was telling me that Control Data was up another *five* points. The emotional aspect came into play.

When you own a stock, you can delude yourself thusly: "This is only temporary, I can't lose any more than I've invested, it still pays a dividend, etc." Sound familiar? With a short position you have no emotional props. You are on margin automatically, and if the trade goes badly, you will be asked for more money. The sky's the limit on price, and you must *pay* any dividends due the person owning the borrowed shares. The emotional turmoil is gut wrenching!

I covered the stock in February 1969 at 169¾. It made it's all-time high of 174 in that period of time, and within one year sold as low as 28¾. Absolutely right but six months early equals a big loss.

Still, there are more compelling reasons not to short: In Chapter 1 we proposed trying for 100 percent gains. The only way this can be done on the short side (without margin) is for the price to go to zero. That is not likely, and even a more normal retracement of 50 percent is only 50 percent of our original investment. If I'm right about the net potential favoring long-term holding, then you're opposing those odds and risking 100 percent or more against that 50 percent potential.

There is one more significant reason: All short sales of stock are considered to be short term, and gains are subject to ordinary income tax provisions.

Trend, timing, emotions, potential, taxes, dividends—all work against you on the short side of the market. It's understandable that there were no bears building mansions in the robber baron era. Virtually every great short-seller in market history returned his wealth to the bulls.

OPTIONS

Ten years ago a primitive market in puts and calls was upgraded to a full-blown options market via the Chicago Board of Options. Small investors were attracted by the gross because of the leverage potential and the easy application of gambling strategies. The game can be played with abandon, showing some spectacular success, and with diversification may allow for a long period of play before the commissions exact their final toll. Let's examine some of the difficulties:

Woody Hayes, the Ohio State University coach, was reluctant to pass the football. His reasoning: "Three things can happen— two of which are bad!"

Options trading could be subjected to the same analysis. If you buy a call, you only make money when the price goes up beyond the strike price. If the stock doesn't change price significantly or it goes down, you lose value in the option; and if it is unsold, you lose the total value at expiration.

Which brings up the next problem. The holding period is carefully defined, and the market prices the option appropriately; so your timing must be impeccable. Eighty percent of all options expire unexercised. You end up buying and selling options from and to other investors and only the brokers benefit.

The current wrinkle is to become a seller of options: You hold IBM, and it's not doing anything. So sell a call on IBM and pocket the money when the option expires. It sounds good, and you may get away with it several times for very small amounts; but sometime the stock will make a major move, and the option buyer will call for it. You've made a few dollars but lost the big ones. You've taken all the risk and lost the corresponding return. And of course there were commissions everywhere.

You're still not convinced? How about an advanced strategy? Strip or strap, straddle, spread, or hedge? We can fix it up so that you're protected whether the stock goes up, down, or sideways. Of course the commissions double—but who's counting? With options, you're playing the purest form of a game of chance. The stocks available for options are institutional favorites—well researched and probably properly priced, with very little chance of finding an undervalued situation here. Everywhere you turn there's zero and double zero and triple zero and . . . no dividends, a poor tax situation, and the average investor can't possibly win. Remember too that the casino closes promptly at 4 P.M. and you ante again tomorrow.

If you own a seat on an options exchange (which nullifies your commission problem), if you have an extremely large bankroll, if you have a computer to calculate the profitable arbitrage levels in advance, and if you play that system consistently, then you may make some money. Too many ifs for me.

COMMODITIES

The dictionary defines commodity as any item of commerce to be bought or sold. This includes grains, fibers, meats, foods, metals, currencies.

There are a number of markets around the country devoted to these agricultural and financial products and their future delivery.

The commodity of primary interest is precious metals—more specifically gold and silver, a traditional haven in times of panic, war, inflation, and other threats to the paper currency and securities. The investor is constantly advised on the buying and selling of gold and silver. The markets are volatile, the margin is low compared to other investments (which seems out of order), and the poorly financed investor is attracted.

Possibly some gold and silver should be held as part of the survival level of your asset pyramid, but speculation in commodities will eventually come to an unhappy ending because of commissions, margin interest, the nonproduction (no dividend) of the commodity, and storage and registration charges. The pluses are use of an inflation hedge, full capitals gains tax treatment (including short sales), and inverse correlation with most financial instruments.

The thing that has kept me out of these markets is the difficulty of evaluation. There are some parallels with corporations (cost of production might be compared to corporate book value, for example).

A number of the methods proposed in this book can be applied to the commodity markets. I just refuse to give up a dividend and have less for evaluation just for a potential hedge. If I'm concerned about the securities market, I lighten up and move toward higher fixed yields or toward stocks that tend to do well in poor markets.

Commodity Futures

Commodity futures involve a contract for future delivery rather than purchase on the spot. The farmer finds this particularly useful to ensure or guarantee a market for his yet unproduced commodity. The speculator gets into the game by trying to guess the future value of the product.

The futures contract is different from the option in that the underlying transaction is mandatory rather than just having the right to force the transaction. To guarantee the future transaction, you are required to put up a deposit bonding you to the transaction. If the trade is moving against you, more deposit will be required or your contract will be traded for whatever the market will bear.

The advantage over spot purchase of commodities is the leverage allowed by only putting up a guarantee deposit rather than the face value of the commodity. Also you're not charged interest on borrowed money. The disadvantage, besides the fact that leverage works both ways, is the percentage impact made on your capital by the commission and the restriction of time in terms of settlement date. Either way there is no dividend.

The market is currently being flooded with index futures. Every commodities exchange in the country wants at least one index for trading. The investor is told that the index future contracts were created to allow hedging of existing portfolio. However, the investor isn't fooled. He knows the "bucket shop" has returned, and he's in there betting for all he's worth, without portfolio!

A one-point move in indexes like Standard & Poor's 500 is $500 gained or lost. Plenty of action for a $5,000 deposit. Two limit days down (6 points) and he has reached the margin maintenance level and must supply additional capital to supplement his now $2,000 equity. There are not many games where you can be wiped out (60 percent of your capital) in two days.

Suppose we play the game the way the brokers (who thought it up) suggest. The minimum contract is 500 units of the index, so for Standard & Poor's that's about $90,000 worth of hedge. We would have to have a portfolio of that size with an average beta of 1 or $45,000 of beta 2. I read recently that 85 percent of Americans do not have $5,000 in financial assets. We've eliminated a lot of investors.

Admittedly no one suggests index futures are for everyone. So perhaps we do have a significant portfolio and want to hedge. To cover our insecurity, we're going to double the commissions and guarantee that we won't make a significant gain because of market movement. It's like playing for a tie in a sports event. If you don't think you're right, why be in the market at this time or play the game at all? By playing for a tie, you're only paying the referees and will never advance to the championship. In my dictionary, hedging is synonymous with losing.

NEW ISSUES

In 1971, Richard Brealey wrote *Security Prices in a Competitive Market* and devoted a chapter to new issues. His thesis was drawn from an analysis of 53 new issues reported in the *Commercial and Financial Chronicle* during the years 1963–65. He concluded that new issues outperformed the general market by 9 percent in the first week after being offered.

Nine percent is significant for such a short period. Always on the alert for a statistical edge, I decided to try it out with real money. I told my broker that I wanted approximately $2,000 worth of each new issue that became available. He didn't object, so we began buying and selling. It didn't take long to discover that I was losing money—good incentive to do the analysis that I should have undertaken earlier. My conclusions were that I wasn't getting a statistically valid sample. Many of the new issues were never offered to me, because they were bought by the office manager, his brother-in-law, etc. I didn't see the popular ones that immediately rose in price on the open market and kept the statistical average high. The stocks that filtered down to me, were the ones not being fought over.

So why not wait until trading begins and buy immediately? First of all, you pay a commission that isn't assessed on the initial offering. Secondly the auction will begin with the good ones well above the offering price. A year ago I subscribed to 100 shares of Key Tronic before it came public. The price wasn't set until the day the trading was to begin. My broker called me shortly after the issue came public at $19.50, and it was already over $26 on the market. I sold it the next day at 26.25, and it's been in decline ever since (7¾ recently).

The underwriter tries to price the stock where the market will accept his supply without his sales staff having to push too hard. If brokers are calling you and offering "new issues," then they are probably under pressure from the management to reduce a bloated inventory. Caveat emptor! With this kind of effort from the underwriter, it's logical that normally there would be more buyers than sellers when the issue starts trading. Brealey's 9 percent is probably representative, but you have to be nimble. Most of the new issues are companies needing money for expansion, having little asset value and probably no earnings—very likely no product to market yet. In short they are normally selling a dream, and it's very difficult to assign a price.

Suppose you like their dream. Let the issue come public, and the market will determine the proper price warranted for company prospects. Watch the stock carefully for a year and if the price stabilizes, start a buying program. Careful positioning as the dream comes to life can bring dramatic rewards. One of my most profitable stocks was Cray Research, and it was accomplished in just that fashion.

Wait until there is some substance. A product, some earnings, market interest. Buying dreams alone can cause nightmares.

MUTUAL FUNDS

The standard advice given to beginning investors by market gurus is to buy mutual funds. For this display of knowledge, these people often make six-figure salaries. Recently they've refined their wisdom by advising no-load mutual funds. That was prompted by a number of studies showing no better—in fact poorer—performance from the load funds.

The reasons for the recommendations are diversification and professional management. In Chapter 6 we demonstrated that diversification eliminates only the unique risk factor and coincidentally the unique "reward" factor, guaranteeing a mediocre or market-indexed performance. A certificate of deposit is almost certain to beat that recommendation.

The broker, ever alert to the decline in interest by the investor, changes the game to bring him back to the casino. Now we have bond funds (including municipal bond funds) and specialized funds stressing the gamut of industries, thereby putting the unique risk back into the investment.

That leaves you with professional management—for a fee of course, which means those funds must be exceptional for the investor to benefit. And every year there are exceptional performances, usually followed the next year by exceptionally poor performances as the character and interests of the market change. Picking last year's best performing fund doesn't work, nor does picking last year's poorest performer.

It's a coin flip (50–50) as to any fund's relative potential from this point forward.

There are some exceptions (John Templeton, for example) that have established themselves over a long period of time. They are still subject to the ups and downs of the market and require a long-term commitment and lots of patience by the investor.

These funds seem stodgy compared to last year's best performance but may average 15–17 percent return to their shareholders.

For me that's not enough. Besides I have several advantages that the fund or institutional manager doesn't have: I am not required by law to diversify my portfolio, so I can assume as much unique risk (and reward) as I desire. I am not required to report on performance on a regular basis, so I can be patient in waiting for a situation to develop or correct itself. Since I am only interested in a handful of stocks, I can learn as much about them as a thousand people can about the entire universe of American corporations.

I don't have the advantage of volume purchases and the corresponding reduction of commissions, but I do have the ability to sell to my best tax advantage. The smaller number of issues also makes it practical to separate years of loss and gain to optimize the capital gains provision.

In recent years the strategy of switching funds (or stress within a fund) has become popular. This lets you make the decision on the type of industry that will be popular next. Usually this can be done with a minimum fee if your fund belongs to a family of funds and specializes in the area of interest that you intend to switch to. If you move to a new fund, then you're subject to the significant spread between bid and asked by the funds, and a couple of switches per year should put you into the negative expectation.

It is recommended that we buy mutual funds for diversification and professional management. Then it is recommended that we select an area of concentration that *we* consider appropriate and switch to a different area when *we* think it will be popular. All you logicians out there work on that, will you?

CHARTING, TRADING, MARKET TIMING

Everyone has heard the old Chinese proverb "A picture is worth a thousand words." When it comes to stock price charts, the more appropriate quotation is, "Beauty is in the eye of the beholder."

The advent of the computer has allowed the tedious process of charting to be more accessible to the average investor. It has resurrected the moribund point and figure methods. The technician is sure that yesterday's price action is giving telltale signs of tomorrow's trading. The academics have again employed their computers to show that all prediction patterns occur naturally when random trading movement is generated. Still, the technical analyst believes. And the Flat Earth Society still meets on a regular basis.

In the late 60s, in my learning phase, I read and tried everything related to stock market speculation. I was interested in Mattel Toys, as was a friend who followed stocks on a technical basis. The chart on Mattel was a classic textbook example of a head-and-shoulders top. We showed the chart to anyone who would look at it, and everyone agreed that the pattern was perfect. We sat drooling as the right shoulder was completed and at the prescribed instant went short. The price continued down briefly (others had the same idea), and then the company made some positive announcement (long since forgotten) and the stock jumped immediately under heavy short covering. I managed to get out in seven days with only a 10 percent loss. Sure, the technical analyst can find historical examples of patterns that work, but I can match each of his with one that fails. Fifty-fifty makes a market.

Technical analysis may be useful in the very short term. I can sit before a ticker tape and by watching each trade and volume level, improve on random selection. However, I have never figured how to overcome the commission drag or the time lag in getting orders executed. Day trading has to be impossible in sustaining profits for the average investor.

If you're in position to get your trades executed immediately at little or no cost and have a large enough bankroll that 15 percent per year warrants devoting your waking hours to the process, then you might try trading. Oh yes, one more thing: you need nerves of steel! Read *The Traders* by Sonny Kleinfield (Holt, Rienhart & Winston). If you're the average investor with $10,000 and a full-time job, two trades a year is maximum unless both are losses. Even then two should be maximum, as the market is telling you something. You're out of step. The way you get back into step is to do some skipping. In my first 15 years of stock trading, I bought and sold 29 stocks in 100 total installments. That's an average turnover of slightly less than 2 per year in a portfolio that averaged three issues. My average loss was held 9 months, and the average gain was 18 months. My commission rate was around 3 percent on an annualized basis.

Most of the investment advice given in market letters and during interviews consists of stock picks and market timing. Everyone has an opinion on which way the market is going, backed by irrefutable evidence. The most asinine comment that the advisor can make is, "I'm out of the market completely!" When and how does he reestablish his position without major error? And what good does that do the average investor, who cannot stand the commission and tax implications? If they say that they are reducing holdings, I'll continue to listen. But show me an advisor that says sell everything, and I'll show you a dummy!

Prices of stocks consist of intrinsic value formed by company prospects and the availability of their basic ingredient—money! On top of value is a layer of psychological expectation created from greed and fear of the investor. Timing requires the ability to anticipate the changing of the psychological mix in the market and the resultant distortion of value in stock pricing.

In the normal state, the stock market represents the collective wisdom of all players and all known information relative to the companies represented. It goes to emotional extremes only once or twice a decade, and a strategy built on timing market excesses will rarely do well. For more on the emotional perspective, read on!

FILTERS AND STOP ORDERS

Earlier we discussed the merits of a buy-and-hold strategy and also a trading strategy. Buy-and-hold is better; but at some point the growth is out of a stock, and stable or declining prices are likely to be the rule. I've mentioned several times that historically the Dow Jones industrials have only grown 4 percent per year. So we must leave a stock at some point. This provokes the question "Is there a mechanical way of leaving a stock?"

Had we been able to anticipate the major advances of this century and avoid only the major declines, we would have had an enormous return. Using the computer it's easy to apply a filter to historical prices and analyze the results. The filter could be some easy rule such as: if the market (or a stock) goes up 20 percent, sell; if it goes down 15 percent, buy. Or you could reverse the rule, selling when it retreats and buying only after an advance.

I employed my computer one entire weekend, seeking the answer to the question, using DJIA data for 65 years. I used all combinations of numbers up and down, trying to improve the 4 percent figure. The best combination raised results to 6 percent. It failed to hold that advantage when used on a different time period. In short, some combinations had to beat the 4 percent (lucky), and some couldn't meet it. There was no evidence that any superiority would last, and 6 percent still isn't good enough to warrant employment.

Now let's turn to the individual stock. Investors are often advised thusly: If a stock goes up 20 percent, sell it or set a stop order 10 percent below the current price and move it up as the stock advances. Pure nonsense on both counts! Why 20 percent rather than 21 or 19? If you're willing to settle for 20 percent gains you'll go broke on 20 percent losses or the additional commissions and taxes that this system will generate.

A stock under random movement needs some room for maneuvering. If placed in a restrictive channel, it's bound to bump into a wall at some point. If the restriction is too loose, then a significant loss will occur when the condition is met.

I have never placed a stop order. I almost always use a limit order on both purchases and sales. My expectations are not as high when selling, as it's a buyer's market.

I leave a stock alone as long as it's performing. If there are signs of weakness, rather than placing a stop order I place a limit order above the current price. I use a high probability factor, depending on the behavior of the stock, but I ask a bonus for selling—not a discount.

CHAPTER 8

Emotional Aspects

I can calculate the motions of heavenly bodies, but not the madness of people.

—*Sir Isaac Newton*

Sir Isaac made his comment after the collapse in 1720 of the South Seas bubble, in which he had invested much of his money. The South Seas Company was venture capitalized to promote trade between England and the South American countries.

The South Seas Company had imitated the French Mississippi Company, established earlier by John Law to bring gold back from the "mountains" of the Louisiana Territory.

Both companies were devoid of assets, without sales or earnings, but would-be investors fought in the streets over each new public offering of stock. At one point the total Mississippi Company stock outstanding was valued beyond the entire gold and silver wealth of France. Finally the paper house collapsed, leaving Newton and others holding the bag.

Such a mania can't be repeated today, right? How about the Florida real estate boom in the 1920s or the two-tiered stock market of the 60s or, more recently, midwest farmland?

During 1984, Washington State had a bankruptcy case where a born-again, C-average, high school graduate collected $58 million from the wheat farmers of eastern Washington for the specified purpose of 2 percent return per week in commodities speculation. No high pressure promotion—the word traveled person-to-person, and would-be investors pursued him over the rural roads, begging him to take their money. The Ponzi method was used, even though the perpetrator had probably never heard of Ponzi. (Incidentally, the originator of the concept of pay the old investors from the donations of the new, thought to be Charles

Ponzi, was really a man named Bianchi. It seems fitting that a system without substance should be named after an alias.)

How can people be so gullible? It isn't a matter of intelligence, as Newton's mind was as fine as the human race has produced. It seems to be the result of psychological factors that can be controlled by the alert investor. Emotion vanquishes intellect! No matter how mechanical and effective the system becomes, it is all for naught unless the emotions are subdued. You may consider my methods the greatest thing since sliced bread, but unless you can put your emotional system in neutral you'll never make it work. I'll have people attend my seminars who'll be lavish in praise, call me regularly for updated wisdom, and then will be steered by a broker into making a decision that doesn't fit anything that I've taught them. Then they call me and cry on my shoulder, even if I had advised them against it earlier. Many people just can't handle the emotions and should never be in the market. The old advice of selling down to the sleeping point would be liquidation for most people.

The most emotional turmoil that I've encountered was my savings and loan lockup. Next in line was a house, in another state, that was being sold that the tenants managed to set on fire and the insurance was in doubt (happily resolved). The only sleep lost due to the stock market was during fall 1974 when margin calls were a regular thing. The problem was not whether I should get out. It was always, "Where do I get the money that will be demanded in the next mail delivery?" I answered them all, contrary to popular advice, and capitalized fully. Today I can have a quarter million of margin in a falling market and not get excited. Remember, it's not bread money, it's just my stock fund!

Let's look at a few of the more common pitfalls and see if we can build some defense mechanisms.

GREED AND FEAR

This dynamic duo creates most of the problems for investors. If you could devise a measure of investor emotion in the form of a ruler, you would mark greed on one end and fear on the other. The balance point would be halfway between, and that is just where investors must position themselves.

Let's deal with fear first. We tend to lose money because we are afraid to lose it! How can you possibly make sound decisions when you're scared to death of the *possible* outcome? Not the probable outcome but the worst case becomes totally unacceptable and distorts your judgment. You must get fear out of the decision process, or you are doomed.

In "Planning Perspective" (Chapter 1), we discussed establishing our speculative fund after our other needs were met and in such a way as to not impact our lifestyle. If you do this rationally before any investments are made, when the emotions are in balance, you'll start with the psychological factors neutralized. Don't get greedy when some initial success occurs and threaten your other assets by adding to the speculative fund. Be disciplined enough to stay with the original planning.

Starting with fear under control, we make each of our investments only after properly studying each issue. Get all the facts you can gather, as knowledge overcomes fear. Forget all opinion, as the market has discounted it in current pricing.

Next simplify and downscale your decisions as much as practical. If you are buying in a poor market, when doom and gloom are everywhere, don't attempt to be perfect; just keep nibbling at the bargains until the market has turned. You can be more rational with each decision, and time is working for you, as there will be a turn. There always has been, and it's very probable that there will be one more.

Try to assign numbers to the decision process. In similar situations in the past, how many times did a decline exceed a certain percentage level? The market is down 15 percent from a previous high. How many times in the last 10 declines was 15 percent exceeded? If less than 5 out of 10, then the odds are in favor of the turn. But it doesn't matter, since *the turn will come* and you will benefit—unless you have a one-stock portfolio and it's the loser of the year. In that case you start again after a short-term tax loss.

Fear occurs in bad times—which seems obvious but needs emphasis to contrast with greed maturing in good times.

The good times may not necessarily be yours. They may be the reported status of your friends, who seem to have all the luck! (Maybe they haven't done as well as reported, since we tend to brag about our successes and suffer our losses in silence.) Regardless you must stay objective and give your investments their deserved opportunity. Start switching now and you're likely to lose both ways. The investments that have performed well will stall, and the laggards will get their day in the spotlight. Every dog has its day! It's all timing; and since you can't predict it, you must wait for your turn to come.

Now your stock is moving, and the temptation is to add to the holdings. Don't do it. The old devil greed is whispering in your ear. After a stock becomes active and increases in price, the end is in sight as the final rush of investors is absorbed. The mathematics are all wrong, and you have to chain your greed.

If you don't add to the holdings, the temptation is still to expect too much from the stock. Use the calendar to regulate your judgment. If the movement has been under way for six months, sell as soon as it is long term and shows any weakness at all. Forget price objectives, as they no longer apply. The psychological attention span of the investor is all that counts at this point.

I mentioned this before, but it is imperative. Don't dip into your other assets (survival or income). Keep these totally separate, as if they belonged to someone else. If you can't do it with the speculative fund in a reasonable period of time, then you can't do it!

Greed and fear—monsters of the market. Keep them locked in their closets, and you'll do well!

GAMBLING FEVER

One of my favorite books is *Wiped Out* by an anonymous investor, published in 1966. It's the story of an investor who started with $62,000 when the Dow was at 485 in October 1957 and was finished in May 1964, when the Dow was at 820, with only $297.78 remaining! It is a classic study of greed and fear—mostly fear— but it also deals with another emotional problem: the desire to play the game!

When I was in college we traveled to track meets in the college station wagon. Two of our athletes spent the entire trip betting on random events (The next service station wil be on the right, No it won't!). They had no interest in accumulation or distribution of wealth—it was strictly for entertainment and bragging rights!

Wiped Out had the same interest. When a stock was doing well, he was anxious to move on to the next one. Always looking for action, he did things just exactly backwards. He cut his gains short and let his losses run. In nailing down a gain, he could brag about his brilliance; but conversely he could never admit to a loss. "It's never a loss until you sell it" was his motto.

Today the index futures attract the person with gambling fever. How can it possibly be thought of as an investment, with no fixed return? The entire profit motive is based on speculation in change of the index up or down. I fail to see any significant difference between futures trading and the racetrack or the roulette wheel. The principal difference is that it can be played from your home, with the phone the only equipment needed.

As long as you find the markets exciting, you're in danger of succumbing to gambling fever. If you can reduce the process to mechanics, then you should be successful following the principles proposed in this book.

You'll know you've washed the gambling fever out of the system when the fun (and the pain) ends. Treat the market like a business with profits, losses, and expenses. If you can't do this, then put your money into certificates of deposit and play the lottery with petty cash. If you must gamble, stay out of the big casino!

MUM'S THE WORD

Earlier I mentioned the book by Murray Bloom and his profile of three winners. No one had the least idea that each of the three had any wealth at all, with the exception of their brokers. They weren't completely isolated from people (not hermits), but even the closest relatives had not a hint of their wealth. They didn't talk stocks with anyone, neither giving nor receiving advice. It was probably a quirk of personality rather than a planned method. Possibly they were worried about being prey for anyone with money needs, as often occurs to the suddenly wealthy.

It is good policy for the serious investor to conduct his operations in secret in order to avoid performance pressure. First of all you have to admit to no one but yourself that you've made a mistake. Take the loss and try again. However, if you've given someone the benefit of your ability to select winners (51 percent—maybe!), won't you be inclined to give the stock another chance rather than admit to your pupil that you've made a mistake?

This is the problem that all brokers have, Rarely will they suggest selling a stock that they've recommended, especially if it hasn't been held long!

If you're worried about what someone else will think about you, it is bound to affect your performance.

I'm really reluctant to recommend stocks, but my friends stay after me until I give in. (Undisciplined!) The problems are:

1. I figure that my selections are as good as the next person's, but I also know that that I've sold 41 percent at a loss.

2. Whatever I'm interested in or would recommend, I've already positioned. It may be a little late for someone else to initiate a program that could be completed for long-term profits.

3. The other person doesn't have my personality or information base, so I don't know how he'll react to setbacks that are bound to occur.

Invariably the person asking for a stock will hold off buying until he sees whether I'm right or not, and he ends up paying more for it when it's farther along in the cycle. I feel obligated to let him know when I'm selling but find out later that he still holds his. He also weights his portfolio differently than I do and may buy very little of what I feel is an exceptional purchase. Conversely he will buy more of stock that I consider highly speculative. Whatever is done, you feel responsible. You wind up worrying more about his stock than your own and usually end up making decisions about your own based on what you think is best for him.

It is a full-time job managing your own investments, so stay out of the advising business, especially if you're not being paid for the information. You'll keep your friends longer if you don't lend them money or give any advice.

THE EXPERT OPINION

As bad as it is to give advice, it's even worse to accept it. We're bombarded with advice from every direction, and ultimately most of it is worth just what we pay for it—nothing! Even if the advice is good we have no way of knowing in advance, so we are much better off to gather our own facts, determine the key issue, plan a retreat if the trade turns sour, and then make our own decision.

This is hard to do when confronted with so much expert opinion. This is the age of the specialist. The definition of specialist that I like best is someone that knows more and more about less and less until he knows everything about nothing.

For most people the broker is the authority figure, and it's very hard for an investor to resist his advice. In my 25 years of stock speculation my brokers have advised me three times and were wrong all three times. The first two times are worth relating.

In January 1963 I decided to buy 100 shares of Control Data for 32.125. That represented nearly 50 percent of my annual salary as an engineer and was a major commitment. Prior to that time I had only purchased six shares of General Electric, and the broker didn't know me from Adam Smith.

But $3,000 was something that he could work with, and he suddenly became my best friend. He called regularly, even though I explained that I had spent it all and expected a long-term investment in honor of my firstborn, who had just arrived.

One day he called with the rumor that Control Data was to be listed on the New York Stock Exchange and advised me that the stock would retreat after the listing was formally announced. He assured me that we could sell the stock with profit and buy it back lower for the long haul. How can you resist such expert advice? Having the normal quota of greed and being extremely busy with my work, I relied on his expertise, and the stock was sold at 36.75 after being held 26 days.

Now the calls came fast and furious. Buy XYZ or PDQ or something else. I reminded him that we were waiting for the pullback in Control Data. Then one day I didn't hear from him, so I was getting my good suit cleaned and pressed, expecting a funeral, when he called.

"You probably wondered where I was yesterday? I visited with the president of a California company, and he assured me that the company was going to do great things. I think you should buy 100 shares of Pacific Vegetable Oil." Control Data had not hesitated and was around 39 by now. The broker assured me that we could make a quick trade in Pacific Vegetable Oil and still get back into Control Data.

So on February 8, 1963 (nine days after selling CDA), we bought 100 shares of Pacific Vegetable Oil at 26.875. On March 4, 1963, I decided on my own to sell Pacific Vegetable Oil at 21.25 and to make my own decisions henceforward.

By the end of 1963, Control Data passed the century mark (par as the old-timers would call it), and Pacific Vegetable Oil was at 8. Pacific Vegetable Oil no longer exists, and Control Data was one of the great stories of the 60s.

What did I learn? The broker talks a good game but rarely plays it any better than you do. Did you realize that 70 percent of the brokers don't own stock? They say it promotes objectivity, but the real reason is that their record cannot stand scrutiny. Why should anyone accept anything other than research and facts from this source?

I also learned to stick with companies that I could evaluate. I understood Control Data. I bought Pacific Vegetable Oil on a rumor, without even a cursory look.

TABLE 8–1 Five Stocks for 1985

Ticker Symbol	Price September 1984	Broker-Estimated Earnings	Other-Estimated Earnings	Beta	5 Percent Inflation Model	Dividend
DEC	$96	$11.85	$8.12	1.25	127	—
IU	18	2.40	1.15	1.10	15.8	$1.20
KPH	16	1.10	.61	.95	7.24	.16
SQB	46	4.40	3.81	.90	42.86	1.44
WMX	40	3.85	3.21	1.15	46.14	.80

The most important thing that I learned was that I had to get the emotions under control. My greed was evident. I was influenced by "expert" opinion and not disciplined enough to stick by my original plan.

One rule evolved from this experience that I never violate: If I receive a broker-initiated call regarding any stock, owned or otherwise, I never decide while the broker is still on his call. I listen carefully, then hang up and let my subconscious mind work the problem. This balances the broker submission. I may call him back with an action. More often than not, questions arise that send me off for further research, with any decision delayed. It is extremely rare that you will miss an opportunity by delaying the reaction to broker-initiated information. Whatever he knows also is known by half the civilized world, and those interested have shaped the first reaction.

Today the investor is deluged with opinion. Your brokerage firm can bury you with opinion, and the market letters, talk shows, books, and magazines make it a seemingly impossible situation.

In September 1984 a major brokerage house published a research report entitled "The Stock Market—Five Stocks for 1985." The timing was superb when I received an unsolicited copy, as I was ready to run a computer workshop where we analyze investment candidates. I chose to use these five stocks for analysis. Since then I've used the same group two more times and plan to continue reviewing these stocks throughout 1985.

The report suggested 9–12 months as the holding period, and exactly nine months after publication of the report a model portfolio with equal amounts of these stocks has gained 3.5 percent without considering commissions and dividends. The DJIA has gained 10 percent in the same period. Tables 8–1 and 8–2 list the stocks and attendant data.

TABLE 8–2 Nine-Month Portfolio Status

Ticker Symbol	Price June 1985	Number of Shares	Portfolio Value	Dividends	Round-Trip Commission	Net Return
DEC	$98.5	20.83	$ 2,051.76	—	$116.36	$ −64.60
IU	14.5	111.11	1,611.10	$100.00	115.45	−404.35
KPH	9.375	125	1,171.875	17.81	110.94	−921.26
SQB	60.125	43.48	2,614.24	50.87	123.75	541.36
WMX	58	50	2,900	30.00	128.70	801.30
Total			$10,348.98	$198.68	$595.20	$ −47.55

The value model column was constructed by the method described in Chapter 4, using consensus estimated earnings of Standard & Poor's and Value Line Investment Services. An expected inflation rate of 5 percent was used. Dividend data was from current estimates, and commissions were computed using the commission model for a full-service brokerage firm described in Chapter 10.

The broker seeking my business had marked with stars his favorite—Key Pharmaceuticals (KPH)!

The portfolio does demonstrate some of my principles. KPH could have been sold prior to long term, and the portfolio would be in much better shape. IU could have been sold short term near 17, although it is the type of stock that I look for. Sold before March 11, a new position could be in progress at this time at lower prices.

I wouldn't have owned DEC (no dividend), and you can see how hard it is to overcome the commission. Note the optimistic earnings estimates of the broker (higher than other estimates at the time).

Even though the losses are significant the other three stocks, while less than spectacular, maintain portfolio value, demonstrating that five stocks are more than enough for mediocre performance.

Unfortunately that is just what we have—a mediocre portfolio. Typical! A service that was consistently bad would be more useful to us, as we could short their picks. This one is not nearly bad enough for that.

The solution to the information problem is to accept facts only—no opinion, no rumors. Study the issues, consider how the stock fits in your plan, make your decision, and review the decision on a regular basis. This is not easy, but there is no other way!

GREATER–FOOL THEORY

Each of us feels that we are smarter than the average investor. Since we are smarter, there is bound to be a buyer willing to take our investment at a higher price when we are ready to sell. This is the attitude we adopt when prices are roaring up day after day and we decide to enter the game. Prices set in motion will tend to remain in motion until some external force is exerted to end the process!

Don't bet on it! The next day's price is like a coin flip. It is said that a coin has no memory, so even if heads have come up 10 times in a row, tails are as likely (50–50) the next time unless the coin is biased.

Investors have memories and know the stock has been going up for months. Everyone is interested, and there are lots of recommendations. Of course there is another set of investors that sees all this as reason to sell, and they start offering their stock to the greater fools coming into the market.

If the stock has been "discovered," it is too late for you. There is no time to position, value has been reached or exceeded, and the odds have shifted against you.

Unfortunately many investors can't resist the attraction of the stock that has already performed. They're like bugs attracted to an electric zapper, with inevitable results. You've got to think in humanitarian terms, as J. P. Morgan did when he said that he was always trying to do his fellow investors a favor by buying their stocks when they didn't want them and selling them back when they did!

This would be considered to be a contrarian approach, and everybody today claims to be a contrarian. One of the few fund managers that I am acquainted with told me when introduced that he was a contrarian (as if I had asked his religion), then proceeded to name his favorite stocks, which were all well-known stocks frequenting the active list.

To be a real contrarian, you have to look through the discard pile and resurrect the real bargains. If you look no further than the active list, then you're the greater fool and I'm looking for you!

THE MADNESS OF CROWDS

In 1895, Gustave Le Bon wrote *The Crowd*, a classic study of sociology. His thoughts are often quoted regarding the behavior of investors and their tendency to act collectively (mental unity), as did the crowds (physically) that Le Bon studied. Quoting directly from *The Crowd*:

> As soon as a few individuals are gathered together they constutite a crowd, and, though they should be distinguished men of learning, they assume all the characteristics of crowds with regard to matters outside their specialty. The faculty of observation and the critical spirit possessed by each of them individually at once disappears.[1]

Later he argues that the collective mental unity does not elevate the wisdom but rather reduces the reasoning:

> This very fact that crowds possess in common ordinary qualities explains why they can never accomplish acts demanding a high degree of intelligence. The decisions affecting matters of general interest come to by an assembly of men of distinction, but specialists in different walks of life, are not sensibly superior to the decisions that would be adopted by a gathering of imbeciles.

The whole matter is laid to rest in one choice comment: "In crowds it is stupidity and not mother wit that is accumulated!"

What this means for the investor is that any time a consensus has been reached, particularly by the experts, it is probably wrong, and your best course of action is to expect the opposite.

In January 1985 the market was boiling along with new highs approaching the 1300 level of the Dow Jones Industrial Average. On the Financial News Network virtually every market analyst predicted an explosion through 1300. A sure thing they said, so I started lightening up, knowing that the consensus had to be wrong. After all, they didn't get that bullish overnight. They obviously had committed their funds and influenced other buying, so who would sustain the rally? The market backed off and four months later has returned to the 1300 level. Things are notably less optimistic now, so I'm encouraged that the market will move onward.

The same principle applies to individual stocks. When you get the same name popping up on everybody's recommended list, it's a prime candidate for sale. When the majority concludes that a company has glowing prospects, the market has already reflected this in the price, and the probability is set for a reversal.

---

[1]Gustave Le Bon, *The Crowd* (New York: Penguin, 1981).

Le Bon says that there are three principles involved with imbuing the "mind" of a crowd with an idea or belief:

1. *Affirmation.* An assertion kept free of all reasoning and proof starts the idea. This has been the basis of religions for centuries.
2. *Repetition.* To create an influence, the idea has to be repeated. This helps fix the idea as a demonstrated truth.
3. *Contagion.* This is where the emotions enter into the process, and the idea spreads rapidly, like a contagious disease. The end result often is panic.

Panic is something the individual investor doesn't need. He quakes in his boots with every little market wiggle, and a full-scale panic puts most small investors on the sideline.

Just exactly the wrong timing. A panic in full bloom creates opportunity that only occurs two or three times in a person's investment life. I would place 1962 and 1974 in that category. Both cases involved a president, and the financial community overreacted. In both cases the "panic" spent itself in about 2 months, with full recovery in less than 15 months. 1929 was obviously the same situation but with a more erratic recovery.

How do you judge the course of a panic? Watch for increasing volume with particular emphasis on institutional selling, gloom-and-doom forecasting, and a predilection for reporting the negative. I like to consult the library archives in those periods, reading old *Wall Street Journals* to see what mood existed at the bottom in 1929, 1962, 1966, 1974, and so on. There were different concerns but the same levels of despair.

Of course panic can work both ways. You can have a buying panic, where everyone is concerned that they will be left behind. Again the institutions usually lead the way, committing the balance of their funds, creating a top to the market.

Do you own thinking on all issues. Le Bon demonstrates that the individual mind is better than the collective mentality of the crowd. If you must seek opinion, use it to form a consensus and then act against that consensus. Too many people agreeing with you is a sure danger sign.

Among animal families it is known that the smarter species are loners. Consider the birds: The least intelligent fly in flocks. The most intelligent, such as the eagle, are solitary. In the case of mammals, the least intelligent are the "cud chewers," which remain in herds. The most intelligent—tigers and foxes—live alone. Learn to stand alone and make your own decisions. Be a fox—not a cow!

Read the history of financial panics and learn from them. The more you know, the less fearful the actual situation becomes. View it as opportunity rather than disaster, since everything comes to an end sometime. It always has!

THE ODD COUPLE: ACTION AND PATIENCE

Do something—even if it's wrong! A tongue-in-cheek witticism that turns out to be very good advice when applied to *buying* stocks.

So many investors study an investment beyond reason and are unable to make a commitment, often passing up real opportunity. They usually compound their mistake by finally taking a full position in the stock after an overvalued state has been reached. You must investigate before investing but then act boldly if the probability is good.

In the stock market, where prices change continually, whatever you do will be wrong—at least for the short term. Once you're committed the stock will be priced above and below what you paid. If it's above, then it's doing what you wanted it to do. If below, it's a better opportunity. Either way you win.

Forget tops and bottoms. You're unlikely to enter or leave at those points, as both represent well less than 1 percent of the stock trades. Anytime you can get the stock below the average trade of the year and sell above the average, you should make money. That's not as difficult to do as seeking turning points. When the fundamentals seem favorable but timing is questionable, make a small commitment and step up the investigative process. Put yourself on a schedule where action is virtually automatic under continuing favorable conditions.

Action pertains mostly to the buying side, as the mechanics discussed in this book should let you out of a stock if you're disciplined enough to watch the calendar on your investments.

Most of our regrets regarding investments center around the fact that we failed to take action—not that we took it. Of course we buy stocks that in hindsight should not have been purchased, and we often sell too soon, as a stock continues to do well. But the big regret is always the missed opportunity or the failure to cut a loss. I believe you can compensate for this by buying in installments to ease the entry decision and using the short-term tax loss to force the exit decision.

The balancing attribute is patience. If you like the company but feel the stock is priced too high, then wait for it to enter your buying range. There are plenty of other stocks, and you should never adopt the attitude that it *must* be this one. Remember that the stock market is basically a buyer's market, and you can't lose money until you invest. Wait for your price. The limit order is the best way to wait. It is unemotional, mathematical, and profitable.

When you're selling you can't be quite as patient. The buyer has the money and the advantage, so you should be more attuned to action.

Once you're committed to a stock and prior to it's performance is when your patience is really tried. As long as it's not creating a significant loss, it must be given time for the situation you envisioned to develop. If it approaches long-term status, you take the tax loss (if there is one) and try again. If there is only a small gain with no visible *increase* in demand (volume), then continue to hold.

Regardless of what many advisers suggest, there is a definite holding period during which you wouldn't buy more but you also shouldn't sell. Often they advise you to consider whether, if you didn't already own it, you would buy the stock at the current price. If the answer is no, then they suggest you sell it. I say they are wrong. For example, I bought Xerox in the 1981–82 period. As usual I was early and the stock continued to decline. I sold the early shares for a short-term loss, and now my entire holdings are profitable. My average purchase price after commission is $36. Today the stock sells for $54. I wouldn't buy shares at that price, because they don't represent 100 percent potential in one year; but neither will I sell yet. I am in the holding period, where the stock is long term and paying off. The dividend can improve your patience remarkably. As long as there is some return on your stock, it's easier to sit with your laggard. You know the dividends are combating inflation and maintaining the purchasing power as long as the stock is not in decline. If it's losing, that's another matter, and you have to take action to preserve your capital.

A very delicate balance has to be struck between acting boldly and exerting patience. Anything that you can do to put this process on a mechanical, unemotional basis will serve you well in your investments.

CHAPTER 9

Communing with Computers

To err is human—it takes a computer to really foul things up.
—*Anonymous*

My favorite computer cartoon shows two cleaning ladies leaning on their mops in a large computer center. One comments to the other: "I've had it explained to me, but I still don't understand it!"

If there's anything that promotes fear in the average person, it's the prospect of confrontation by a computer. People are literally forced into using this remarkable tool.

It's not that tough to understand, but it is difficult to describe. My introduction to computers came during college in 1958, when only a handful existed in the world. The college hired a German national who was doing original work in prime number theory to be our first instructor.

After sitting through a few lectures in broken English on the internals of his program, we sought outside counsel, which consisted of one book. With the book in hand and the computer available on weekends (no one else knew how to use it!), we muddled through.

Today the bookshelves are loaded with introductions to this tool, and classes are readily available through all sources of community instruction. Anyone with career ambitions had better get acquainted now, as the computer is everywhere.

I realize that computers will complicate an already complex theory, but I believe that I'm experienced enough to teach you and that you are intelligent enough to grasp the concepts. Chapter 10 will provide the incentive needed, as these programs can simplify and improve your investing.

HELP FROM THE HOME COMPUTER

No product in history has undergone the level of advertising hype that has accompanied the introduction of the personal computer. Early sales were to professional people who understood its use and had a demonstrated need. Sales soon followed to status seekers or those brainwashed by salespeople, with visions of cultural shock or the bread lines for their children if not in possession of the personal computer. The initial wave of enthusiasm is now gathering dust on desks or in closets, as the limited use of the computer becomes apparent.

The computer doesn't solve every problem. Many things are still best done by hand (e.g., recipes). Most people are not disciplined enough to organize and record data. The game-playing craze has passed, and Junior has plenty of access to computers at school. So what function do they have beyond paperweighting or stimulating conversation?

The two principal areas of individual application are the preparation of written material (word processing) and spreadsheet analysis. The spreadsheet process can be useful to the small-business person or to the investor, as can other specifically prepared applications. Still, the current state of computers for the investor is analogous to high-quality stereos with a limited record selection. The records (programs) that are available are excellent but aren't always just what the user wants to hear. More on this later!

Let's look at investor needs by five categories: database, accounting, statistical, technical, and analytical. There are some programs that don't fall neatly into these categories, but they will serve to relate your needs to possibilities.

First is database access. Through a phone linkup to one of several database services, you can access current price quotations or financial data on a selective basis. Complete ticker service is available. In addition most have news items and historical data accessible. Some even have book material on file. Data can be screened by a number of variables and transferred to your local, smaller database for further analysis. For example, you could list all stocks with price-earnings ratio (P/E) less than 10 and beta of 1.2 or greater. Principal vendors are *Value Line Investment Survey*, Dow-Jones News/Retrieval, The Source, and Compuserve. Most require a registration or subscription fee plus charges for minutes used. Phone hookup, disc storage, and 64k memory are required.

In the accounting area, spreadsheet programs such as Lotus 1–2–3, Visicalc, and others allow the general solution of many investment problems without programming per se. This would include but not be limited to financial report analysis, portfolio status, performance analysis, and tax recording and preparation. Many of these applications exist as special-purpose programs at less expense and with smaller machine requirements than necessary for spreadsheet analysis.

Statistical methods are necessary to modern portfolio theory (MPT) and are available from virtually all vendors of hardware. The standard statistical software package costs less than $50, will run on a 16k machine, and requires no discs, printers, modems, or other expenses. Most packages offer simple linear regression with correlation analysis and descriptive statistics, including mean and standard deviation. These routines are invaluable for measuring risk, combining stocks to minimize risk, and evaluating options. They are described in Chapter 10.

Tehnical evaluation and trading programs are beautiful applications of a computer because of the volumes of data involved and the need for dynamic analysis and reanalysis. Graphical presentation or charting is more complicated, expensive, and very machine dependent, thus limiting the access for the individual unless you have the specific machine required. The technical approach is of most importance to high-volume, in-and-out trading with vehicles such as commodities futures. Many sophisticated commercial packages are available with elaborate graphics—if you have the right machine and the money. The individual investor can use simple time series methods (e.g., moving averages), without visuals, for simple trend extension in prices, earnings, and so forth.

The fifth and final cluster would be the vast category of analytical or modeling programs. This group of routines, if properly used, is the most useful and the least demanding of resources. The smallest machine without printer, disc drives, or modem is adequate. Fifty dollars worth of computer is sufficient.

The list of analytical programs is open ended but is typified by time-value-of-money calculation. This would include compound interest, present-value bond models, annuties, amortization, sinking funds (IRAs), etc. The model concept extends to earnings or dividend-based stock pricing and options, limit order buying probabilities, advanced-option strategies, tax planning, commission calculation, net worth forecasting, yield analysis, market timing, and others. The model is an attempt to simplify and simulate reality as an aid to the decision process.

As mentioned earlier most "canned" programs won't entirely satisfy the user. The investment problem, with the exception of graphics, is fairly easy to program, and investors should consider taking 10–20 hours of introductory BASIC programming, enabling the writing of simple procedures or modification of existing ones.

BUYING A COMPUTER

In buying a computer for investment purposes there are very few requirements. If you have additional need outside the investment arena, then that will normally dictate the type and size of the machine. Word processing or spreadsheet analysis will require a specific brand and size of machine to run the particular package that interests you. This means an expensive machine in addition to the software packages.

If you don't already have a computer and are only interested in investment applications, then you can buy a Commodore VIC 20 for less than $50 that will allow use of the programs in Chapter 10. Addition of a $40 tape unit provides the semipermanent storage that negates the need to rekey the program each time it is to be used.

You might consider the first $50 to be an educational expense. This allows you to try out some of the programs and see if there is long-term benefit to your investment program. After some experimentation, you might add storage (tape or disc) or opt for a more sophisticated machine encompassing other use.

Although I'm not attracted to databases, you may want to screen stocks, which means a telephone connection and disc storage to retain the selected data. I prefer to enter my data via keyboard, using the *Value Line Investment Survey* from the local library. As you probably recognize by now I don't spend an unnecessary dollar. Some people would call that cheap, but I call it thrifty!

Another consideration might be the used-computer market. There are a number of good personal computers, long since discontinued, hiding in closets around the country. The Texas Instruments TI99–A is a prime example. Watch for these to be advertised or seek one through your own advertising.

The computer can be deducted as an investment expense but must now be depreciated, where it was once immediately deductible. Check with your tax accountant before declaring the deduction.

If your first machine is the least expensive available, then you might consider it a throwaway as you experiment to see how it might be useful to you.

THE ANATOMY AND PHYSIOLOGY OF COMPUTERS

Today virtually everyone is familiar with the handheld calculator. It differs only slightly from the computer, and most investors have of necessity become acquainted with it. The difference between the two machines is storage capacity and control. Use of either tool requires a sequence of instructions to be accomplished upon a collection of data. In using the calculator, the instruction sequence is normally stored in, and controlled by, the human mind, and the data usually is stored on paper along with the answers produced.

The instruction sequence for a calculator is minimal, usually consisting of simple arithmetic operations. Take the difference of stock prices (subtract), divide by the first price and multiply by the 100 to get percentage change, for example. The computer has a wider range of instructions that it can perform, both arithmetic and logical. But the most significant advantage that the computer has is the ability to store within itself both instruction sequences (called programs) and data used in, and resulting from, the execution of the program sequence. This idea of "stored program" goes back to the mid-1940s and is attributed to John Von Neumann.

The computer is organized physically around logical components: input/output, storage, arithmetic/logical operations, and control.

In both calculator and computer, input is mostly via a keyboard. For the computer there are sometimes intervening devices, such as a card or optical readers, but most input is via keying. Output is normally on a display with some form of printer (often attached to produce a permanent record) on both machines.

Storage on a computer can be temporary or semipermanent. A working memory, where instructions and intermediate calculations are stored, is cleared whenever the machine has the power removed, as with the calculator. However, magnetic tape or disc can be used to save information for future use, regardless of power considerations. The recording is done through magnetic pulses, just as music is recorded on the same medium. Names are given to the programs and to each piece of data so that they may be located and reused in the future.

The power of the computer and its difficulty in use are in the prepared set of instructions that can describe extensive calculation. It permits repetition on changing data that can reduce years of hand calculations to seconds.

The pioneering work in numerical weather prediction was accomplished by Lewis Fry Richardson during World War I. He was a pacifist (Quaker) working as an ambulance driver. While awaiting business near the battlefields, he would occupy his time in hand calculation of a one-day forecast of atmospheric motion. He spent 20 some years of his life on the single weather forecast, and it turned out to be unrealistic because of the inaccuracies of the measured data used.

Richardson envisioned great orchestras of people calculating under the control of a conductor to keep the data synchronized. Today computers are doing just exactly that, making relatively accurate forecasts in a matter of minutes. Try doing a regression analysis by hand and then let the computer do it. The advantage becomes evident.

The computer can manipulate the data submitted to it but can also manipulate its own instructions. It can test for various conditions and alter the sequence of instructions executed. The data can consist of simple numerical values, defined to be continually reused in that form (constants) or as values to be altered by the program or the user (variables). The constants are identified in the programs (example—7.57) and are always found in that form. Variables are given names (A, B, X, Z1 . . .) and altered as the occasion demands. A person's height might be referred to as X and would be 68 for one person and 73 for another.

Nonnumerical data, used as text or as labels, can be stored either as constants or as variables, with the definitions discernible to both the user and the computer, classified as either "numeric" or "string."

The computer is approached in either a compose or an execute mode. The human communicates with the computer through the keyboard by using "action" keys or composing a message.

The action keys are wired to create an immediate activity by the computer. There are normally three of these:

1. The RESET button, or key, initiates a start-again reaction that will destroy the program in temporary memory and

return control to the operating system. This is used only as a last resort.

2. The BREAK key stops (interrupts) any execution and returns the initiative to the human.

3. The ENTER or RETURN key sends the last message on the display to the computer to be saved or executed, depending upon the mode employed.

As you develop the instructions needed to solve a problem, you subject your work to extensive alteration until the process behaves as you envisioned it working. This period of program development is termed debugging. When you think the program is ready, you instruct the computer to try it out by submitting an execution command, such as RUN. The computer will start at the beginning of the program and execute each instruction in turn, as encountered. Often, this literal interpretation of your instructions creates some undesired action, and you must correct the program by reentering the composition phase. Most computers have a BREAK key to return control to the compose phase. The entire process is analogous to constructing an elaborate shopping list, editing it, and when it is complete going to each of the stores indicated for the listed action.

In composing each message or instruction to the computer, mistakes will be made. If discovered prior to submission to the computer, they may be corrected by simply retyping the portion in error or using editing procedures built into the language. Once the statement is complete, it is submitted to the computer via the ENTER key (or a facsimile).

When the set of instructions is complete, a unique name is given to the program, and some variation of the SAVE command is used to copy the program onto the semipermanent storage medium of tape or disc. Retrieval of that program for future use is done with the command LOAD, followed by the same name given when the program was SAVEd.

This duplicates the program from the semipermanent storage into the temporary memory. Turning off the machines will destroy the temporary version but not the semipermanent (disc or tape) copy.

You may clear the temporary memory with the word *NEW* in preparation for entry of a new program. After you key each program in Chapter 10 and if you have tape or disc storage capacity, SAVE with a unique name (or number) and then enter NEW before keying the next program. Otherwise you may end up with a mixture of two programs, neither of which will work properly. Even if you don't save the program it must be cleared before any additional key-in is made.

The computer can make no real distinction between instructions and data. It is all coded and recorded numerically on the machine. If told to execute an instruction in a certain area of memory, the computer will attempt it unless the instruction code is unrecognizable.

To protect against this and other housekeeping problems, each computer has a management program called an operating system. This program is always in temporary memory as you work with your instructions, simplifying the logistics of handling data and preparing instructions.

Additionally, since the computer is basically stupid and understands a very limited range of instructions, another program has been developed to interpret the English language for the computer. This allows you to work in a subset of English called BASIC (Beginners All-Purpose Symbolic Instruction Code), which is then reduced to the simple instructions the computer uses.

For every instruction the user prepares for the computer, hundreds of others are executed in finding and labeling data, controlling the execution phase, and breaking general instructions into detailed sequences.

INSTRUCTIONS TO THE OPERATING SYSTEM

The following key words or commands are understandable to most operating systems and manage the logistics of an investor preparing and submitting programs to the computer. There may be some simple word substitution on your computer. If the commands don't work as indicated, consult the reference manual prepared by the vendor of your machine.

BASIC This instruction indicates the language that the program expects in order to communicate. Some machines only understand the one language and thus don't need the instruction. My computer is an early Radio Shack version, and the BASIC interpreter is on the machine when I turn it on. Most machines must have it requested.

LOAD "name" This command initiates a search of the directory for the program named between the quote marks. The name must be spelled precisely, with no breaks inserted, usually eight characters or less in length. Be careful not to confuse the letter O and the number 0.

RUN Instruction to begin execution of the program just fetched by a LOAD command or just keyed by the investor. The process starts at the lowest-numbered BASIC statement (see next section).

SAVE "name" Any BASIC instructions that are in temporary memory are written to semipermanent memory (tape or disc), and a directory is prepared to aid future retrieval and use.

NEW Clears the temporary memory in preparation for keying a new program. When keying the programs of Chapter 10, give each a unique name (P1, P2, P3, etc.) and follow the last statement in each program with a SAVE "P1" (or whatever the name). After the SAVE is complete and the machine quiet, follow with a NEW to clear memory in preparation for Program 2 (P2).

LIST As you prepare your investment program, it is good practice occasionally to review the instructions that have been given to the machine. This command will show you the program sequenced in the order specified by statement numbers.

ELEMENTS OF THE BASIC LANGUAGE

Computer languages are not the free-flowing communications that humans use to express themselves. It's more like talking to a very small child or a dog. Emphasis is on key words, with some simple symbolism supplementing the action to be taken.

The BASIC constructs are these: statement numbers, verbs, variable names, constants, operators (arithmetic, relational, and logical) combined into expressions and functions.

The statement number is the first thing necessary to producing a computer instruction. It must be unique and appear in the numerical sequence where you plan to have it performed. The numbers can range from 1 to 10,000 or more, depending on the dialect of the language for your machine. You'll notice that I usually start with 10 and increment by 10. This leaves plenty of room for insertion of additional instructions later. The numbers don't need to be consecutive, but must be in order.

If you try to reuse a number, it will result in destroying (redoing) the original statement. This is convenient when you want to change it but disastrous when unintended.

Following the statement number is the action verb. These are words such as INPUT, PRINT, LET, GOTO, IF. The word must be as precisely spelled as commands to your dog have to be properly enunciated (SIT, STAY, ROLL OVER).

The remainder of the statement supplements the verb and takes on a different form for each statement. It may describe variables or constants to be acted on.

As mentioned, variables describe a memory location where data are temporarily stored as work is performed. When finished, a new entry may be made into the variable. Constants may be used in the statement directly, without any further concern about their status.

Let's put all this together in the following statement:

100   LET A = 2 * B

LET is the key word (verb). A and B are variables. We don't know what B is before this statement, but statement 100 will multiply whatever is stored there by 2 and will replace the value in Variable A with the result. The number 2 is a constant. The = means complete the action on the right and then place or assign the result to the location specified on the left.

The 2 * B is an expression, and the various possibilities in building expressions and then repeating them, propagates the power of the computer. Arithmetic operators include add (+), subtract (−), multiply (*), divide (/), and exponentiate ([). Expressions can be subdivided into partials by enclosing in parentheses, or they may be placed in separate lines. They may also appear in PRINT statements. The following examples create the same result:

Example 1:

100   A = B * C/E + P * Q

Example 2:

100   A = (B * C/E) + (P * Q)

Example 3:

100   X = B * C/E
110   Y = P * Q
120   A = X + Y

The equal sign (=) also specifies a logical comparison for testing purposes. If you want to count a process, you can use a variable (example, I), increment it each time the process is repeated, and then test to see if the desired number has occurred. For example:

```
10   I = I + 1
20   IF I = 10 THEN STOP
```

IF, THEN and STOP are verbs that will halt the process when the value found in I has progressed to a value of 10 (explained later in this chapter).

The programs discussed in Chapter 10 make extensive use of logical relationships to determine the proper course of action to be taken.

Relational operators include:

=   The constants, variables, and arithmetic appearing to the left of the = are compared to the constants, variables and arithmetic appearing to the right of the = sign for equality.

<>   These two characters symbolize and test for the exact opposite condition sought by the = sign (not equal).

< (less than)   This symbol, pointing to the left means that a positive reaction occurs when results of the expressions to the left are smaller than the expressions on the right.

> (greater than)   Opposite of the previous symbol. Reacts to larger on the left.

<=   Less than or equal to.

>=   Greater than or equal to.

These relationships can be combined logically for multiple conditions. For instance, you might seek stocks with P/E less than 10 and dividend yield greater than 5 percent. The entire expression would be written (PE < 10) * (DY > 5), where PE is price-earnings ratio and DY is dividend yield.

The logical operator * means AND (both relations must be true for the test to be satisfied).

The other logical operator is + (OR), which means if either relationship is true, then the test is satisfied and positive action is taken.

The remainder of the language consists of punctuation. The comma and parentheses are used to separate or group, respectively. Quote marks identify messages or labels that are to appear precisely as given. The colon and semicolon organize the statement for the computer.

This will be less confusing when we introduce a complete example. The intent here was to define any elements used in my working programs.

ELEMENTARY PROGRAMMING CONCEPTS

The computer normally operates sequentially until the sequence is interrupted. The ability to test and interrupt without human intervention makes quick solutions to large problems. To understand programs, you must understand the concepts associated with control of computer processes.

First let's look at a simple, straightforward sequence designed to calculate simple interest using the formula $i = prt$, familiar to most elementary students. Let's assume a rate (r) of 12 percent (.12) and a holding time (t) of three years and allow the principal (p) to be given by the user. The following example applies:

```
10   INPUT P
20   LET I = P * .12 * 3
30   PRINT I
```

Very simple! Statement 10 calls for the principal to be given during execution of the program. This is done by the computer, displaying a ? after the RUN is entered. The computer pauses until a principal value is keyed and the ENTER key depressed. The rate and time are constants. Statement 30 will display the result of the computation on the monitor. The program is executed in three steps (10, 20, 30) and then stops. If you wish to execute a second time with the new principal, then you execute RUN again and introduce the new principal when the computer pauses after printing ? or equivalent. The INPUT verb allows the human to intervene with new or additional data.

Now suppose that we have a number of principal values to run through the program and want to avoid having to resort to the execution each time. We can add:

```
40   GOTO 10
```

This transfers control at the end of the sequence to the beginning of the sequence, and the process is automatically repeated. This is termed a loop, and in theory the program now will never end but will continue to ask us for a new principal value. When we finish we just walk away from it.

Suppose we want to vary the rate of return or the holding period. Also, how do we remember in the future what the question mark means? The following program is more complete and useful:

```
10   PRINT "ENTER PRINCIPAL IN DOLLARS"
20   INPUT P
```

```
30   PRINT "ENTER RATE AS A FRACTION"
40   INPUT R
50   PRINT "ENTER TIME OF INVESTMENT IN YEARS"
60   INPUT T
70   LET I = P * R * T
80   PRINT "TOTAL INTEREST PAID WILL BE ";I
90   GOTO 10
```

To this point, we haven't demonstrated the true power of the computer. In fact we've just duplicated the calculator process. Now let's look at something more complex—compound interest!

When programmers analyze a problem to be solved by the computer, they usually like to draw a picture of the logic involved. This picture is called a flowchart. Figure 9–1 demonstrates the logic of computing compound interest. The variable I keeps track of the number of times the interest is computed and fed back into the process. Q is the compounding multiplier that will eventually adjust the principal. P and R are as defined for our simple interest problem. N is time in number of years.

Note the diamond-shaped box containing I : N. This is shorthand for compare I to N. If I < N (less than), then continue the calculation. When I reaches the exact value of N, multiply the principal by Q and display the result.

This testing to determine a change in sequence is called a "branch." In the BASIC language an IF verb is used, followed by the relationship being tested, followed by the modifier THEN, which is followed by another action verb.

The program appears in Figure 9–2. If you have a computer, test the program, using a principal of $1,000, rate of interest .105, for an investment of 20 years. The result should be $7,366.21 if the program is keyed properly.

Note that the program of Figure 9–2 only compounds once per year. A version that compounds as frequently as desired appears in Chapter 10 (Program 6–1). Even annual compounding is tedious to accomplish on a calculator; daily compounding is virtually impossible.

Some of the programs require data to be stored in table form while the program is executing. Tax tables, commissions, etc., are stored, using data-handling elements of the language.

The data is defined, using DATA statements. At the point where the data is needed a READ is executed to search the table for the line of data needed. The results are transferred to the

FIGURE 9–1   Compound Interest Flowchart

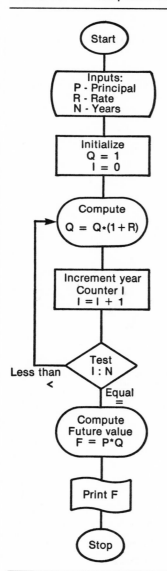

variables listed following the READ. When finished with the search a RESTORE is executed to return the table pointer to the beginning.

If the table entries vary they may be given to the program by the user as an "array." I've used the variable name A to hold these

---

FIGURE 9–2 Compound Interest Program

```
10   PRINT "ENTER PRINCIPAL IN DOLLARS"
20   INPUT P
30   PRINT "ENTER RATE AS A FRACTION"
40   INPUT R
50   PRINT "ENTER TIME OF INVESTMENT IN YEARS"
60   INPUT N
70   LET Q = 1
80   LET I = 0
90   LET Q = Q * (1 + R)
100  LET I = I + 1
110  IF I < N THEN GOTO 90
120  LET F = P * Q
130  PRINT "FUTURE VALUE IS ";F
140  END
```

---

values and the DIM statement to indicate the maximum space needed. If I am finding the mean of eight heights given to me, I will store them in $A(1)$, $A(2) \ldots A(8)$ for later use. If I have asked the computer to reserve 1,000 spots using DIM A(1000), most of the space will be unused but may be needed at another time. If I want to refer to all values, then I can index my way through them with a variable counter, for example, $A(I)$. For example, to find which of the eight people is 68 inches tall, I might do the following:

```
10   LET I = 0
20   LET I = I + 1
30   IF A(I) = 68 THEN STOP
40   IF I < 8 THEN GOTO 20
50   PRINT "NO ONE IS 68 INCHES"
```

You'll find it very difficult to write programs with the brief explanation given here, but it should prove useful in working with the models in Chapter 10. If you want to develop your own programs, take a BASIC course at your local college.

VENDOR VAGARIES

Even though most computers operate under the BASIC interpreter, there are a number of dialects—which creates some problems in writing programs that will execute on more than one computer.

The programs of Chapter 10 have been written with some of these problems in mind, and a major effort was made to avoid use of idioms peculiar to only part of the available computers. For some of you, that means extra keying, as I've avoided shortcuts. For example, some computers allow multiple actions per line, which compresses the program and simplifies key-in. Others allow the PRINT and INPUT to be combined into an INPUT with lables—again reducing key-in.

There are some elements, if unavailable, that create significant extension of the instructions. For example, the use of exponentiation (power) symbols ([↑ ^ or **) if unavailable on your machine necessitates having one of the substitutions documented in Appendix B. Even with the care I've used, there are a number of things you should be aware of.

Size restrictions: Most restrictions rarely come into play, but you should be aware of the possibility. Statement length on my computer is limited to 64 characters, but some computers allow less. If you encounter this, break your long statement into smaller multiple units or abbreviate labels. Variable names have been kept to one character if possible, although most machines allow two or more (which gives variety and better description).

The string variables on my machine can only be A$ or B$. No other name can be used. You may encounter machines that won't allow strings at all. Since my machine only allows them as labels (they haven't been tested), all you would lose is some description in your results.

The size of a constant varies with machines, and all computers must resort to a shorthand notation to use extremely large or small numbers. If there are more than six digits in the number, then the scientific (exponential) notation is used. This consists of the most significant digits of the number, followed by a multiplier that allows proper placement of the decimal point.

As example, the number 123456. can be used as is. However, the number 1234567. must be entered and will be displayed as 1.23457E + 06. Note that commas are not allowed, except to separate numbers. Note also that in reducing from seven to six digits, the low order 67 was turned into 7(0). This is called rounding and may vary somewhat from machine to machine, creating slight variation in results. If using the programs from Chapter 10 creates slightly different answers than found in my examples, it may be due to round-off. The E + 06 tells the computer that the decimal point needs to be shifted six places to the right. For fractions the exponent may need to be shifted left. Example: .000123456 will be used as $1.23456E-04$. Minus is left, plus is right.

In order to begin a report with a clear display, I have used a CLS verb. This is an acronym for clear screen. Not all vendors accept this. Apple uses HOME to do the same thing. Check your reference manual and make the appropriate substitution if necessary.

Since my computer has no printer (That's right—seven years without a printed line!) all output has been directed to the display. If you want to redirect your output to a "hard copy," then change the appropriate PRINT verb to LPRINT or add another line substituting LPRINT as the verb. The same applies to listing the program for a printed copy. Use LLIST rather than LIST.

Because of all the differences in using disc or tape for storing data, I've avoided anything but key-in (INPUT) and display (PRINT). If you're familiar with use of tape or disc, then you may want to modify Program 1–1 to store data permanently.

CHAPTER 10

Computer Models

We can easily represent things as we want them to be.
—Aesop

This is the era of the computer model. Any self-respecting investment expert has and heeds his computer models. Ask him how the model works and often he'll tell you that the formula is proprietary (read secret). This adds an aura of mystery that makes you think the computer is smarter than the man. There isn't a computer existing that improves on human thought processes, although work on artificial intelligence has gone on for decades. The chess masters still routinely beat the computers.

What the computer does do is fast and accurate calculation of the tedious variety that humans are likely to avoid or do poorly. For the investor, just the organization of data in preparation of feeding the computer will enhance his decision making. You don't ask the computer to decide anything; just use it to compress the data into information.

The models discussed in this chapter align with the methods of the first six chapters and are numbered accordingly. I include only those that I've found to be useful. See Appendix A for the complete listings of programs referred to in the text by number. If you want to extend your interest I recommend the book by William Riley and Austin Montgomery cited in Appendix C. Since the methods have been discussed earlier, I'll confine the description to examples that will allow you to check and use the programs that interest you.

TIME VALUE OF MONEY AND YIELD ANALYSIS

The eight programs (6–1 through 6–8) in this series are very similar, as they all deal with the compounding of money over time.

Starting with compound interest, a few simple modifications change it into bond value models or the interest payment on your house. You'll notice I've used the same statements in several of the programs, which could simplify the initial key-in.

Compound Interest (6–1)

A $1,000 principle invested for 5 years and compounded quarterly at 12 percent interest would generate the following dialogue:

COMPUTER	INVESTOR
PRESENT VALUE OR PRINCIPAL IS?	1000
NUMBER OF YEARS FOR INVESTMENT? .	5
ANNUAL PERCENTAGE RATE OF INTEREST?	12
NUMBER OF TIMES COMPOUNDED EACH YEAR?	4
FUTURE VALUE USING COMPOUND INTEREST IS 1806.11	

Present Value of Zero-Coupon Bond (6–2)

Assuming the bond to be worth $1,000 at maturity, what should the bond be worth at today's interest rates? Remember, the bond is discounted because interest is part of the face value to be paid at maturity.

COMPUTER	INVESTOR
FUTURE VALUE OR PAR IS?	1000
NUMBER OF YEARS FOR INVESTMENT?	5
ANNUAL PERCENTAGE RATE OF INTEREST?	12
NUMBER OF TIMES COMPOUNDED PER YEAR?	2
PRESENT VALUE OF ZERO-COUPON BOND IS 558.395	

Present Value of Bond (6–3)

Since bond coupons are fixed for the life of the bond, the market adjusts the bond price to changing interest rates. This program will help determine the current market value of the coupon bond, using as an example a bond issued at 10 percent when current yield on comparable bonds is 12 percent.

COMPUTER	INVESTOR
FUTURE VALUE OR PAR IS?	1000
COUPON AMOUNT RECEIVED EACH PERIOD?	50
NUMBER OF YEARS FOR INVESTMENT?	5
ANNUAL PERCENTAGE RATE OF INTEREST?	12
NUMBER OF TIMES COMPOUNDED EACH YEAR?	2
PRESENT VALUE OF COUPON BOND IS 926.40	

Annuity/Amortization Payment (6–4)

Annuities and amortization involve exactly the same process, differing only in who holds the money. If you've established your money in an annuity, then you get paid. If the bank has loaned the mortgage on your house, then you pay the amortization. For a $50,000 mortgage over 25 years at 14 percent the monthly payment is found as follows.

COMPUTER	INVESTOR
PRESENT VALUE OF PRINCIPAL IS?	50000
NUMBER OF YEARS FOR INVESTMENT?	25
ANNUAL PERCENTAGE RATE OF INTEREST?	14
NUMBER OF PAYMENTS EACH YEAR?	12
AMORTIZATION PAYMENT IS 601.882	

Sinking Fund/IRA (6–5)

The sinking fund has been popularized in recent years as the individual retirement account. Deposit $2,000 each year and watch your retirement fund grow. For the example assume a $500 quarterly contribution for 25 years and assume the average rate over that time to be 11 percent.

COMPUTER	INVESTOR
NUMBER OF DEPOSITS MADE EACH YEAR?	4
AMOUNT DEPOSITED EACH PERIOD?	500
NUMBER OF YEARS FOR INVESTMENT?	25
ANNUAL PERCENTAGE RATE OF INTEREST?	11
NUMBER OF TIMES COMPOUNDED EACH YEAR?	12
FUTURE VALUE OF SINKING FUND IS 267512	

Interest Rate from Present and Future Values (6–6)

This program is useful to derive the compounded rate when told how a certain principal has grown over the years: Warren Buffett's $1 to $30 in 13 years, for example!

COMPUTER	INVESTOR
PRESENT VALUE OR PRINCIPAL IS?	1
NUMBER OF YEARS FOR INVESTMENT?	13
FUTURE VALUE OR PAR IS?	30
NUMBER OF TIMES COMPOUNDED EACH YEAR?	1
INTEREST RATE IS 29.9047	

Yield-to-Maturity (6–7)

The coupon yield of an investment shows what the original investment earns. However, we are interested in the dynamic, or market, yields. The current yield is the annual coupon amount divided by the current price of the investment. This tells you what the market value of your money is earning. A third yield of concern to bond investors is the yield-to-maturity. This involves averaging the price between current market value and the eventual par value at maturity. Our example is a 13.5 percent coupon.

COMPUTER	INVESTOR
FUTURE VALUE OR PAR IS?	1000
NUMBER OF YEARS TO BE INVESTED?	25
COUPON AMOUNT RECEIVED EACH PERIOD?	67.50
MARKET VALUE OF SECURITY?	1180
YIELD-TO-MATURITY PERCENTAGE IS 11.7248	

Yield-to-Call (6–8)

In recent years we have the happy situation of bonds yielding so well that the issuing agents are recalling the paper and reissuing at lower rates. This usually means some form of incentive to the investor holding the paper. He will get a premium beyond the par value, and the issuing authority will pay the commission to the brokers. The investor is being offered this routinely for bonds issued in the 1980–85 period. Using the bond example for yield-to-maturity and assuming you will be paid market value (1180) for a bond that can be called in four years without commission (now or later), you're interested in the yield to a call of 107 that will be forced in four years. The question is, can you better the rate by cashing in now? Current compounding bond yields are 10 percent.

COMPUTER	*INVESTOR*
FUTURE VALUE OR PAR IS?	1000
COUPON AMOUNT RECEIVED EACH PERIOD?	67.50
MARKET VALUE OF SECURITY?	1180
CALL PRICE OF BOND?	1070
NUMBER OF YEARS UNTIL BOND IS CALLABLE?	4
YIELD-TO-CALL PERCENTAGE IS 9.55556	

TAX AND COMMISSION PLANNING

To be successful in the stock market, you must watch taxes and commissions carefully. Know the effect that each has on your investment before you take any action.

Ideally you should run through the 1040 tax form two or three times prior to the end of the tax year. However, a program to aid this becomes obsolete quickly, as tax rules, tables, etc., change annually and new instructions and forms are not usually available until after the tax year ends.

So, to simplify the tax problem but still have a useful tool, I've included two programs: One takes you through Schedule D for capital gains/losses analysis; the other works the estimated tax from Form 1040–ES.

Schedule D (6–10) is not likely to change, except for the exclusion rates (60 percent long-term gain, 50 percent long-term loss). If the law is changed, then the appropriate fractions should replace .60 and .50 in statements 410, 440, and 460.

The estimated tax program (6–9) will need some change each year. Statements 1–16 comprise the table for joint return for 1985 (see Table 10–1). Note that it is in reverse order and has been padded with lines of zero at the end. This allows for variation in table size from year to year and a maximum of 16 entries. If the table must be enlarged beyond that or if you want to shorten it (if tax simplification becomes law), then change statement 250 to reflect the new length.

TABLE 10–1 1985 Tax Rate Schedule Y: Married Filing Joint Return

Over	But Not Over	The Tax Is	Of the Amount Over
$ 0	$ 3,540	$ 0	
3,540	5,720	0 + 11%	$ 3,540
5,720	7,910	239.80 + 12%	5,720
7,910	12,390	502.60 + 14%	7,910
12,390	16,650	1,129.80 + 16%	12,390
16,650	21,020	1,811.40 + 18%	16,650
21,020	25,600	2,598.00 + 22%	21,020
25,600	31,120	3,605.60 + 25%	25,600
31,120	36,630	4,985.60 + 28%	31,120
36,630	47,670	6,528.40 + 33%	36,630
47,670	62,450	10,171.60 + 38%	47,670
62,450	89,090	15,788.00 + 42%	62,450
89,090	113,860	26,976.80 + 45%	89,090
113,860	169,020	38,123.30 + 49%	113,860
169,020	—	65,151.70 + 50%	169,020

You must replace this table each year with the appropriate schedule applicable to your status. You must also change statement 20 to reflect the appropriate minimum deduction defined in line 2 of the worksheet.

Statement 130 computes the total exemptions using this year's value of 1040. This must be changed for each new tax year.

Tax planning is most effective when you can compare two years, with some option as to stocks that may be sold in either year.

Tax Planning (6–9)

The first entry requested by the program is adjusted gross income. You add all your income, less exclusions and deferrals. Make any legitimate adjustments for business or moving expense, retirement plans, alimony, etc. See page 1 of the 1040. For the example, we'll use $25,000.

Next enter the expected total of itemized deductions from Schedule A. Use $5,600 to test the program. Assume five exemptions, and the dialogue looks like this:

COMPUTER	INVESTOR
ENTER ADJUSTED GROSS INCOME?	25000
ENTER AMOUNT OF ITEMIZED DEDUCTIONS?	5600

(*COMPUTER*)	(*INVESTOR*)
ENTER NUMBER OF EXEMPTIONS?	5
TAXABLE INCOME IS 17740	
TAX IS 2007.6 BRACKET IS 18	
PRESS ENTER TO CONTINUE?	

Schedule D (6–10)

To use this program, you should itemize your gains and losses on Schedule D. An old form will probably work, as little other than date changes from year to year.

COMPUTER	INVESTOR
ENTER SHORT-TERM GAINS OR LOSSES—ONE AT A TIME?	
IDENTIFY OR DESCRIBE PROPERTY?	IBM
PRICE RECEIVED AFTER COMMISSIONS?	10527.16
PROPERTY COST INCLUDING COMMISSIONS?	13218.37
NET PROFIT/LOSS IS −2691.21	
ENTER 999, WHEN FINISHED WITH SHORT-TERM TRADES?	999
SHORT-TERM NET IS −2691.21	
ENTER ANY SHORT-TERM LOSS CARRYOVER?	162.50
NET SHORT-TERM GAIN OR LOSS IS −2853.71	
ENTER LONG-TERM GAINS OR LOSSES—ONE AT A TIME?	
IDENTIFY/DESCRIBE PROPERTY?	NONE
PRICE RECEIVED AFTER COMMISSIONS?	0
PROPERTY COST—INCLUDING COMMISSIONS?	0
NET PROFIT/LOSS IS 0	
ENTER 888, IF FINISHED WITH LONG-TERM TRADES?	888
LONG-TERM NET IS 0	
ENTER ANY LONG-TERM LOSS CARRYOVER?	1200
NET LONG-TERM GAIN OR LOSS IS −1200.00	
NET GAIN OR LOSS IS −4053.71	
MAXIMUM CAPITAL LOSS IS −3453.71	
SHORT-TERM LOSS CARRYOVER IS 0.00	
LONG-TERM LOSS CARRYOVER IS 0.00	

FULL–SERVICE AND DISCOUNT COMMISSIONS (6–11)

Commissions will vary with the brokerage firms, and the full-service and discount tables used in this program may not be totally representative of your brokerage firm. The program should serve as a planning tool, demonstrating the difference in commission percentage based on the number of shares and price range.

COMPUTER	INVESTOR
ENTER NUMBER OF SHARES?	100
ENTER PRICE PER SHARE?	23.25
ESTIMATED COMMISSIONS BASED ON JULY 1985 RATES	
FULL-SERVICE COMMISSION IS 64.225 FOR 2.76237 PERCENT	
DISCOUNT COMMISSION IS 49 FOR 2.1075 PERCENT	

LIMIT ORDER ANALYSIS

Use of the limit order is thoroughly discussed in Chapter 5. The computer application consists of three programs: The first computes a volatility factor, the second the limit order price; the third estimates combination probabilities.

Percentage Change Computation (5–1)

This program averages the day-to-day percentage change in price to give a representative unit change. The amplitude of the change is of interest, not the direction. The prices must be recent to be representative, and at least 20 days are needed to give statistical validity to the process. The resulting number is not beta. Beta is a ratio of stock price standard deviation to the standard deviation of an index. Value Line beta may be used in the calculation of limit order prices but may not be as realistic as current price history.

COMPUTER	INVESTOR
NUMBER OF QUOTATIONS TO BE ENTERED?	21
ENTER CLOSING PRICE?	12.75
ENTER CLOSING PRICE?	12.25
ENTER CLOSING PRICE?	12.125
ENTER CLOSING PRICE?	12.25
ENTER CLOSING PRICE?	11.875
ENTER CLOSING PRICE?	12
ENTER CLOSING PRICE?	12.125
ENTER CLOSING PRICE?	12.5
ENTER CLOSING PRICE?	13.125
ENTER CLOSING PRICE?	13
ENTER CLOSING PRICE?	13.125
ENTER CLOSING PRICE?	13.25
ENTER CLOSING PRICE?	14.125
ENTER CLOSING PRICE?	13.75
ENTER CLOSING PRICE?	13.25

(*COMPUTER*)	(*INVESTOR*)
ENTER CLOSING PRICE?	13.25
ENTER CLOSING PRICE?	12.875
ENTER CLOSING PRICE?	12.875
ENTER CLOSING PRICE?	12.625
ENTER CLOSING PRICE?	12.625
ENTER CLOSING PRICE?	12.375
AVERAGE DAILY PERCENTAGE CHANGE IS 2.08673	
ESTIMATED BETA FOR PRICE CALCULATION IS 1.30421	

Limit Order Prices (5–2)

This is the principal program as it determines the actual price to be entered on the limit order, based on the desirability of owning the stock. You may use the result of the percentage change computation or Value Line beta to represent unit change.

COMPUTER	INVESTOR
ENTER CURRENT QUOTATION IN DOLLARS AND CENTS?	12.375
INDICATE USE OF AVERAGE % CHANGE(1) OR VALUE LINE BETA(2)?	1
ENTER AVERAGE PERCENTAGE CHANGE?	2.08673
ENTER 1 TO BUY STOCK OR 3 TO SELL?	1
ENTER NUMBER OF TRADING DAYS ALLOWABLE, MAXIMUM 30?	10

CURRENT PRICE	AVG. % CHANGE	TRADING DAYS
12.375	2.08673	10

PROBABILITY	LIMIT PRICE	VARIATION	PERCENTAGE
10	10.8953	−1.47967	−11.9569
20	11.2052	−1.16979	−9.45287
30	11.4118	−.963208	−7.78349
40	11.5926	−.782445	−6.32278
50	11.7346	−.640417	−5.17508
60	11.8508	−.524212	−4.23606
70	11.9541	−.420919	−3.40136
80	12.0659	−.309105	−2.49780

PRESS ENTER TO RESTART?

Combinatorial Probability (5–3)

This allows you to package multiple bids at various probabilities of success in order to have a high probability of partial success with significant discounts. If bids are entered concurrently, then beware of the possibility of more than one purchase!

COMPUTER	INVESTOR
NUMBER OF STOCKS TO BE BID?	3
ENTER PROBABILITY FOR STOCK 1?	50
ENTER PROBABILITY FOR STOCK 2?	40
ENTER PROBABILITY FOR STOCK 3?	30
COMBINATORIAL PROBABILITY IS 79 PERCENT	

MATHEMATICAL STATISTICS AND MODERN PORTFOLIO THEORY

The methods of Chapter 3 have been adapted for the computer in the next two sections. The examples of that chapter can be used to test your programs after key-in on your computer.

Descriptive Statistics (3–3)

The standard deviation requires the square root of the variance. This occurs at statement 260. The up arrow (↑) or bracket ([) indicates an exponential operation. The square root is the ½, or .5, exponential power. If your machine can't handle the exponential notation, then consult the substitutions in Appendix B. Table 3–1 entries are used as an example.

COMPUTER	INVESTOR
ENTER ONE POINT AT A TIME,USE 99999 AS LAST VALUE?	77
ENTER ONE POINT AT A TIME,USE 99999 AS LAST VALUE?	68
ENTER ONE POINT AT A TIME,USE 99999 AS LAST VALUE?	69
ENTER ONE POINT AT A TIME,USE 99999 AS LAST VALUE?	67
ENTER ONE POINT AT A TIME,USE 99999 AS LAST VALUE?	72
ENTER ONE POINT AT A TIME,USE 99999 AS LAST VALUE?	68
ENTER ONE POINT AT A TIME,USE 99999 AS LAST VALUE?	67
ENTER ONE POINT AT A TIME,USE 99999 AS LAST VALUE?	69
ENTER ONE POINT AT A TIME,USE 99999 AS LAST VALUE?	99999
MEAN IS 69.625	
STANDARD DEVIATION IS 3.37798	

Inferential Statistics (3–4)

This program should give you no trouble at all in entry or execution on your computer and could well become the most useful of all the computer applications. You can use it to investigate cause and effect, independence of price movement in two stocks, computation of beta, and so on.

The only caution is to enter data as pairs. The independent value (X) is followed by the dependent value (Y), separated by a comma. In correlation studies, either stock could be chosen as X or Y. In computing beta, enter the index value as X.

Table 3–5 is used as example in the following dialogue to compute beta.

COMPUTER	INVESTOR
ENTER DATA IN PAIRS (X,Y)—END WITH 999,999?	19,46
ENTER DATA IN PAIRS (X,Y)—END WITH 999,999?	8,−6
ENTER DATA IN PAIRS (X,Y)—END WITH 999,999?	−12,16
ENTER DATA IN PAIRS (X,Y)—END WITH 999,999?	9,−22
ENTER DATA IN PAIRS (X,Y)—END WITH 999,999?	10,42
ENTER DATA IN PAIRS (X,Y)—END WITH 999,999?	18,30
ENTER DATA IN PAIRS (X,Y)—END WITH 999,999?	−13,−25
ENTER DATA IN PAIRS (X,Y)—END WITH 999,999?	−23,−57
ENTER DATA IN PAIRS (X,Y)—END WITH 999,999?	44,−4
ENTER DATA IN PAIRS (X,Y)—END WITH 999,999?	23,33
ENTER DATA IN PAIRS (X,Y)—END WITH 999,999?	−13,−19
ENTER DATA IN PAIRS (X,Y)—END WITH 999,999?	3,21
ENTER DATA IN PAIRS (X,Y)—END WITH 999,999?	11,23
ENTER DATA IN PAIRS (X,Y)—END WITH 999,999?	21,0
ENTER DATA IN PAIRS (X,Y)—END WITH 999,999?	999,999
ALPHA IS −.860773	
BETA IS .85762	
R-SQUARE IS .269558	

EQUITY VALUATION

The programs discussed in this section will help assess a company's financial quality, forecast earnings, and place an estimated value on share prices.

Financial Report Analysis (3–1)

The program analyzes the balance sheet and the income statement to produce some of the financial ratios discussed in Chapter 3. The 1984 Annual Report for Xerox Corporation was used as example.

COMPUTER	INVESTOR
ENTER DATA IN MILLIONS OR THOUSANDS FOR CONVENIENCE	
ENTER NAME OF COMPANY?	XEROX
ENTER TOTAL COMMON SHARES OUTSTANDING?	95.7
ENTER CURRENT PRICE OF COMMON PER SHARE?	54
ENTER CURRENT ASSETS?	3739.2
ENTER CURRENT LIABILITIES?	2451.1
ENTER INVENTORY VALUE?	1300.0
ENTER TOTAL ASSETS?	9537.1
ENTER LONG-TERM LIABILITIES?	1614.3
ENTER PREFERRED STOCK AT PAR VALUE?	442
ENTER VALUE GIVEN TO INTANGIBLES?	0
ENTER NET INCOME FOR THE YEAR?	290.5
FUNDAMENTAL ANALYSIS FOR XEROX	
WORKING CAPITAL IS 1288.1	
CURRENT RATIO IS 1.52552	
QUICK RATIO IS .995145	
BOOK VALUE IS 52.557	
BOOK/PRICE RATIO IS .973277	
EARNINGS PER SHARE IS 3.03553	
PRICE/EARNINGS RATIO IS 17.7893	
RETURN ON EQUITY IS .0577569	

Moving Averages (3–2)

Using Table 3–2 as the example, data are entered one point at a time, giving 9999 as a last entry to signal the computer that all data has been entered. The program can be used for a variety of technical methods, from 200-day moving averages to relative strength. The example uses the routine to project (forecast) next year's earnings based on systematic growth in earnings for the past 10 years.

COMPUTER	INVESTOR
ENTER ONE POINT AT A TIME, USE 9999 AS LAST VALUE?	2.71
ENTER ONE POINT AT A TIME, USE 9999 AS LAST VALUE?	3.16
ENTER ONE POINT AT A TIME, USE 9999 AS LAST VALUE?	3.80
ENTER ONE POINT AT A TIME, USE 9999 AS LAST VALUE?	4.18
ENTER ONE POINT AT A TIME, USE 9999 AS LAST VALUE?	3.07
ENTER ONE POINT AT A TIME, USE 9999 AS LAST VALUE?	4.51
ENTER ONE POINT AT A TIME, USE 9999 AS LAST VALUE?	5.06
ENTER ONE POINT AT A TIME, USE 9999 AS LAST VALUE?	5.77
ENTER ONE POINT AT A TIME, USE 9999 AS LAST VALUE?	6.69

(COMPUTER)			(INVESTOR)
ENTER ONE POINT AT A TIME, USE 9999 AS LAST VALUE?			7.33
ENTER ONE POINT AT A TIME, USE 9999 AS LAST VALUE?			9999
NUMBER OF POINTS TO BE AVERAGED?			3
PERIOD	VALUE	AVERAGE	
1	2.71	2.71	
2	3.16	2.935	
3	3.80	3.22333	
4	4.18	3.71333	
5	3.07	3.68333	
6	4.51	3.92	
7	5.06	4.21333	
8	5.77	5.11333	
9	6.69	5.84	
10	7.33	6.59667	
PREDICTED VALUE IS 8.08667			
PRESS ENTER TO CONTINUE?			

Sharp's Value Model (4–1)

Use the $8.09 earnings estimate found from moving averages (3–2) and a beta of .85762 found from regression of Xerox against the Dow Jones Industrial Average. A current inflation rate of 4 percent gives the following estimate of intrinsic value for Xerox.

COMPUTER	INVESTOR
ENTER ANNUAL EARNINGS?	8.09
ENTER BETA?	.85762
ENTER INFLATION RATE?	4
MODEL VALUE IS 99.1164	

PORTFOLIO MANAGEMENT

These programs allow you to analyze your past transactions or to evaluate current holdings.

Performance Analysis (1–1)

This program automates the procedure described in the last section of Chapter 1. The program is most useful when transactions can be saved on disc or tape and supplemented when new transactions are completed. However, this is difficult to describe in a general way for the variety of computers and their data management requirements, so I've avoided the problem by using starter values to reflect the previous transactions. These starter values are utilized in statements 1–13 by rekeying the entries for each statement, using the last printed data from previous execution of the program. For example, you would change statement 1 from LET DD=0 to LET DD=4.18083E+06 after completing the example given.

In order to simplify the program significantly, holding periods are input rather than transaction dates. If your computer has a spreadsheet capability, this process might be better accomplished using it. The real advantage of using the computer is the need to organize your records and the insight that this provides.

Using the example in Chapter 1 but restricting input to one gain and one loss will give the following results.

COMPUTER	*INVESTOR*
ENTER NUMBER OF SHARES—0 WHEN FINISHED?	200
ENTER STOCK IDENTIFICATION?	MERRILL
ENTER NUMBER OF DAYS STOCK WAS HELD?	124
ENTER PRICE PER SHARE PAID FOR STOCK?	15.75
ENTER COMMISSION AND FEES FOR PURCHASE?	74.65
ENTER PRICE PER SHARE RECEIVED FOR STOCK?	15.
ENTER COMMISSION AND FEES FOR SALE OF STOCK?	63.36
ENTER TOTAL DIVIDENDS PAID ON STOCK?	110

MERRILL

TOTAL GAIN	PERCENTAGE	ANNUAL RATE
−178.01	−5.52029	−16.2492

ENTER NUMBER OF SHARES—0 WHEN FINISHED?	300
ENTER STOCK IDENTIFICATION?	WESTERN
ENTER NUMBER OF DAYS STOCK WAS HELD?	690
ENTER PRICE PER SHARE PAID FOR STOCK?	17.875
ENTER COMMISSION AND FEES FOR PURCHASE?	117.17
ENTER PRICE PER SHARE RECEIVED FOR STOCK?	28.125
ENTER COMMISSION AND FEES FOR SALE OF STOCK?	89.36
ENTER TOTAL DIVIDENDS PAID ON STOCK?	735

WESTERN

TOTAL GAIN	PERCENTAGE	ANNUAL RATE
3603.47	65.7607	34.7865

ENTER NUMBER OF SHARES—0 WHEN FINISHED?	0

WINS	LOSSES	ANNUAL %	OPTIMAL BET %
1	1	29.9054	338.986

AVG. GAIN %	AVG. LOSS %	GAIN DAYS	LOSS DAYS
65.7607	5.52029	690	124

(COMPUTER)			*(INVESTOR)*
NET RETURN	COMMISSIONS	DIVIDENDS	
3425.46	344.54	845	

THE FOLLOWING NUMBERS REPLACE THE STARTER VALUES IN
STATEMENTS 1–13, RESPECTIVELY, OF THE PROGRAM

4.18083E+06	1.25029E+08	1	1
3425.46	344.54	845	690
124	−3224.65	5479.67	−178.01
3603.47			

Portfolio Status (5–4)

This program looks at your current portfolio to compute dollar value. If you use margin the program will analyze the equity status and alert you to the level of expected margin calls.

For the example, we'll assume that we have two stocks: 1,000 shares currently priced at 9.375 and 500 shares at 27.25. Our margin debt is $7,214.36.

COMPUTER	*INVESTOR*
ENTER NUMBER OF SHARES OF ONE STOCK—0 WHEN FINISHED?	1000
ENTER CURRENT PRICE OF ONE SHARE?	9.375
ENTER NUMBER OF SHARES OF ONE STOCK—0 WHEN FINISHED?	500
ENTER CURRENT PRICE OF ONE SHARE?	27.25
ENTER NUMBER OF SHARES OF ONE STOCK—0 WHEN FINISHED?	0
ENTER DEBT?	7214.36
CURRENT PORTFOLIO VALUE IS 23000	
CURRENT EQUITY IS 15785.6	
FIRM MARGIN EXCESS IS 4285.64	
BUYING POWER IS 8571.28	
LEVEL WHERE EQUITY REQUIRED 10306.2	
PERCENTAGE CHANGE FROM CURRENT LEVEL 55.1903	

PROGRAM 1–1 Performance Analysis

```
  1   LET DD=0
  2   LET RD=0
  3   LET NW=0
  4   LET NL=0
  5   LET NR=0
  6   LET TC=0
  7   LET TD=0
  8   LET WT=0
  9   LET LT=0
 10   LET LR=0
 11   LET WR=0
 12   LET TL=0
 13   LET TW=0
 15   PRINT "ENTER NUMBER OF SHARES—0 WHEN FINISHED"
 20   INPUT N
 30   IF N=0 THEN GOTO 370
 40   PRINT "ENTER STOCK IDENTIFICATION"
 50   INPUT A$
 60   PRINT "ENTER NUMBER OF DAYS STOCK WAS HELD"
 70   INPUT Z
 80   PRINT "ENTER PRICE PER SHARE PAID FOR STOCK"
 90   INPUT P
100   PRINT "ENTER COMMISSION AND FEES FOR PURCHASE"
110   INPUT F
120   PRINT "ENTER PRICE PER SHARE RECEIVED FOR STOCK"
130   INPUT V
140   PRINT "ENTER COMMISSION AND FEES FOR SALE OF
      STOCK"
```

Performance Analysis (*continued*)

```
150   INPUT H
160   LET G = N*V − H
170   LET E = N*P + F
180   PRINT "ENTER TOTAL DIVIDENDS PAID ON STOCK"
190   INPUT X
200   PRINT A$
210   PRINT "TOTAL GAIN","PERCENTAGE","ANNUAL RATE"
220   LET W = G − E + X
230   LET R = (365/Z)*100*W/E
240   PRINT W,W*100/E,R
250   LET DD = DD + E*Z
260   LET RD = RD + E*Z*R
270   IF W>0 THEN GOTO 310
275   LET LR = LR − E
280   LET NL = NL + 1
285   LET TL = TL + W
290   LET LT = LT + Z
300   GOTO 330
310   LET NW = NW + 1
315   LET WR = WR + E
320   LET WT = WT + Z
325   LET TW = TW + W
330   LET NR = NR + W
340   LET TC = TC + F + H
350   LET TD = TD + X
360   GOTO 15
370   PRINT "WINS","LOSSES","ANNUAL %","OPTIMAL BET %"
380   LET R = RD/DD
390   LET P = NW/(NW + NL)
400   LET Q = TL/LR
410   PRINT NW,NL,R,R*P/(R/100 − P + 1)/Q
420   PRINT "AVG. GAIN %","AVG. LOSS %","GAIN DAYS","LOSS
      DAYS"
430   PRINT TW/WR*100,Q*1OO,WT/NW,LT/NL
440   PRINT "NET RETURN","COMMISSIONS","DIVIDENDS"
450   PRINT NR,TC,TD
460   PRINT "THE FOLLOWING NUMBERS REPLACE THE STARTER
      VALUES"
470   PRINT "IN STATEMENTS 1−13, RESPECTIVELY, OF THE
      PROGRAM"
480   PRINT DD,RD,NW,NL,NR,TC,TD,WT,LT,LR,WR,TL,TW
```

PROGRAM 3–1   Financial Report Analysis

```
  5  PRINT "ENTER DATA IN MILLIONS OR THOUSANDS FOR
     CONVENIENCE"
 10  PRINT "ENTER NAME OF COMPANY"
 20  INPUT A$
 30  PRINT "ENTER TOTAL COMMON SHARES OUTSTANDING"
 40  INPUT C
 50  PRINT "ENTER CURRENT PRICE OF COMMON PER SHARE"
 60  INPUT P
 70  PRINT "ENTER CURRENT ASSETS"
 80  INPUT A
 90  PRINT "ENTER CURRENT LIABILITIES"
100  INPUT L
110  PRINT "ENTER INVENTORY VALUE"
120  INPUT I
130  PRINT "ENTER TOTAL ASSETS"
140  INPUT T
150  PRINT "ENTER LONG TERM LIABILITIES"
160  INPUT Z
170  PRINT "ENTER PREFERRED STOCK AT PAR VALUE"
180  INPUT V
190  PRINT "ENTER VALUE GIVEN TO INTANGIBLES"
200  INPUT X
210  PRINT "ENTER NET INCOME FOR MOST RECENT YEAR"
220  INPUT Y
230  PRINT "FUNDAMENTAL ANALYSIS FOR ";A$
240  PRINT "WORKING CAPITAL IS ";A − L
250  PRINT "CURRENT RATIO IS ";A/L
260  PRINT "QUICK RATIO IS ";(A − I)/L
270  LET B = (T − X − L − Z − V)/C
280  PRINT "BOOK VALUE IS ";B
290  PRINT "BOOK/PRICE RATIO IS ";B/P
300  PRINT "EARNINGS PER SHARE IS ";Y/C
310  PRINT "PRICE/EARNINGS RATIO IS ";P/(Y/C)
320  PRINT "RETURN ON EQUITY IS ";Y/C/B
```

PROGRAM 3–2   Moving Averages

```
 10  DIM A(1000)
 20  LET P = 0
 30  PRINT "ENTER ONE POINT AT A TIME, USE 9999 AS LAST
     VALUE"
```

Moving Averages (*continued*)

```
 40   LET P=P+1
 50   INPUT A(P)
 60   IF A(P)<>9999 THEN GOTO 40
 70   LET P=P−1
 80   PRINT "NUMBER OF POINTS TO BE AVERAGED"
 90   INPUT N
100   PRINT "PERIOD","VALUE","AVERAGE"
110   LET Q=0
120   LET I=0
130   LET I=I+1
140   LET M=0
150   IF I>N THEN GOTO 220
160   LET L=0
170   LET L=L+1
180   LET M=M+A(L)
190   IF L<I THEN GOTO 170
200   LET A(I+P)=M/I
210   GOTO 270
220   LET L=I−N
230   LET L=L+1
240   LET M=M+A(L)
250   IF L<I THEN GOTO 230
260   LET A(I+P)=M/N
270   LET Q=Q+1
280   IF Q>11 THEN GOTO 600
290   PRINT I,A(I),A(I+P)
300   IF I<P THEN GOTO 130
310   LET X=A(P)+A(2*P)−A(2*P−1)
320   PRINT "PREDICTED VALUE IS ";X
600   LET Q=0
610   PRINT "PRESS ENTER TO CONTINUE"
620   INPUT A$
630   PRINT "PERIOD","VALUE","AVERAGE"
640   GOTO 290
```

PROGRAM 3–3   Descriptive Statistics

```
 10   DIM A(1000)
 20   LET Z=0
 30   LET P=0
 40   LET S=0
```

Descriptive Statistics (*continued*)

```
 50   PRINT "ENTER ONE POINT AT A TIME,USE 99999 AS LAST
      VALUE"
 60   LET P=P+1
 70   INPUT A(P)
 80   IF A(P)=99999 THEN GOTO 200
 90   LET S=S+A(P)
100   GOTO 50
200   LET P=P-1
210   PRINT "MEAN IS ";S/P
220   LET I=0
225   LET I=I+1
230   LET X=A(I)-S/P
240   LET Z=Z+X*X
250   IF I<P THEN GOTO 225
260   PRINT "STANDARD DEVIATION IS ";(Z/(P-1))[.5
270   GOTO 20
```

PROGRAM 3–4 Inferential Statistics

```
 10   LET X=0
 20   LET Y=0
 30   LET N=0
 40   LET S=0
 50   LET T=0
 60   LET U=0
 70   PRINT "ENTER DATA IN PAIRS (X,Y)—END WITH 999,999"
 80   LET N=N+1
 90   INPUT C,D
100   IF (C=999)*(D=999) THEN GOTO 200
110   LET X=X+C
120   LET Y=Y+D
130   LET S=S+D*D
140   LET T=T+C*C
150   LET U=U+C*D
160   GOTO 70
200   LET N=N-1
210   LET P=X/N
220   LET Q=Y/N
230   LET B=(U-N*P*Q)/(T-N*P*P)
240   LET A=Q-B*P
250   LET R=(A*Y+B*U-N*Q*Q)/(S-N*Q*Q)
```

Inferential Statistics (*continued*)

```
260   PRINT "ALPHA IS ";A
270   PRINT "BETA IS ";B
280   PRINT "R-SQUARE IS ";R
290   LET W=U−X*Y/N
300   IF W<0 THEN PRINT "INVERSE"
310   GOTO 10
```

PROGRAM 4–1 Sharp's Value Model

```
900   PRINT "ENTER ANNUAL EARNINGS"
910   INPUT E
920   PRINT "ENTER BETA"
930   INPUT B
940   PRINT "ENTER INFLATION RATE"
950   INPUT I
960   LET V=E*B*100/(I+3)
970   PRINT "MODEL VALUE IS ";V
980   GOTO 900
```

PROGRAM 5–1 Percentage Change Computation

```
1100   PRINT "NUMBER OF QUOTATIONS TO BE ENTERED"
1110   INPUT N
1120   LET S=0
1125   LET I=0
1130   LET I=I+1
1140   LET X=Q
1150   PRINT "ENTER CLOSING PRICE"
1160   INPUT Q
1170   IF I=1 THEN GOTO 1190
1180   LET Y=Q−X
1184   IF Y<0 THEN LET Y=−Y
1188   LET S=S+Y/X
1190   IF I<N THEN GOTO 1130
1200   PRINT "AVERAGE DAILY PERCENTAGE CHANGE IS ";S*100/
       (N−1)
1205   PRINT "BETA FOR PRICE CALCULATION IS ";S*100/(N−1)/
       1.6
1210   GOTO 1100
```

PROGRAM 5–2 Limit Order Prices

```
 10   DATA 3.80,1.60,1.29745,1.02379,.776169,.552219
 20   DATA 2.85,1.35,1.09473,.863824,.654892,.465935
 30   DATA 2.30,1.10,.892,.703857,.533616,.379651
 40   DATA 1.85,.85,.689273,.543889,.41234,.293366
 50   DATA 1.5,.65,.527091,.415915,.315319,.224339
 60   DATA 1.25,.45,.364909,.287941,.218297,.155312
 70   DATA .95,.35,.283818,.223954,.169787,.120798
 80   DATA .6,.3,.243273,.191961,.145532,.103542
 82   RESTORE
 84   CLS
100   PRINT "ENTER CURRENT QUOTATION IN DOLLARS AND
      CENTS"
110   INPUT P
120   PRINT "INDICATE USE OF AVERAGE % CHANGE(1) OR
      VALUE LINE BETA(2)"
125   INPUT K
127   IF (K<>1)*(K<>2) THEN GOTO 120
130   IF K=1 THEN GOTO 520
132   IF K=2 THEN GOTO 550
140   PRINT "ENTER 1 TO BUY STOCK OR 3 TO SELL"
150   INPUT T
160   IF (T<>1)*(T<>3) THEN GOTO 140
170   PRINT "ENTER NUMBER OF TRADING DAYS ALLOWABLE—
      MAXIMUM 30"
175   INPUT D
190   IF D>30 THEN LET D=30
200   CLS
210   PRINT "CURRENT PRICE","AVG. % CHANGE","TRADING
      DAYS"
220   PRINT P,B,D
230   PRINT
240   PRINT "PROBABILITY","LIMIT PRICE","VARIATION",
      "PERCENTAGE"
250   LET C=.01
260   LET E=D/5
265   IF E<1 THEN GOTO 280
270   LET E=E-1
275   GOTO 265
280   LET L=D/5-E
300   LET I=0
305   LET I=I+1
310   LET S=0
```

Limit Order Prices (*continued*)

```
320   LET X=0
330   LET U=0
350   LET K=0
355   LET K=K+1
370   READ X
380   IF U=1 THEN GOTO 410
390   IF K>L THEN GOTO 600
400   LET S=S+X
410   IF K<6 THEN GOTO 355
420   LET W=(T−2)*B*S*C*P
430   LET V=(T−2)*B*.33*C*P
440   IF S<1 THEN LET V=V*S
450   LET Q=P+W+V
460   LET F=(Q−P)/P*100
470   PRINT I*10,Q,Q−P,F
480   IF I<8 THEN GOTO 305
490   PRINT "PRESS ENTER TO RESTART"
500   INPUT A$
510   GOTO 82
520   PRINT "ENTER AVERAGE PERCENTAGE CHANGE"
530   INPUT B
540   GOTO 140
550   PRINT "ENTER VALUE-LINE BETA FACTOR"
560   INPUT B
570   LET B=B*1.6
580   GOTO 140
600   LET U=1
630   LET G=0
640   LET Z=D−5*L
650   IF Z=0 THEN GOTO 700
660   LET J=0
665   LET J=J+1
670   LET G=G+.217*X
680   LET H=H−.0085
690   IF J<Z THEN GOTO 665
700   LET X=G
710   GOTO 400
```

PROGRAM 5–3   Combinatorial Probability

```
800   PRINT "NUMBER OF STOCKS TO BE BID"
810   INPUT N
```

Combinatorial Probability (*continued*)

```
820   LET P=1
830   LET I=0
835   LET I=I+1
840   PRINT "ENTER PROBABILITY FOR STOCK ";I
850   INPUT S
860   LET P=(100-S)/100*P
870   IF I<N THEN GOTO 835
880   PRINT "COMBINATORIAL PROBABILITY IS ";100-P*100;"%"
890   GOTO 800
```

PROGRAM 5–4   Portfolio Status

```
600   LET P=0
610   PRINT "ENTER NUMBER OF SHARES OF ONE STOCK—0
      WHEN FINISHED"
620   INPUT S
630   IF S=0 THEN GOTO 680
640   PRINT "ENTER CURRENT PRICE OF ONE SHARE"
650   INPUT Q
660   LET P=P+Q*S
670   GOTO 610
680   PRINT "ENTER DEBT"
690   INPUT D
700   PRINT "CURRENT PORTFOLIO VALUE IS ";P
710   PRINT "CURRENT EQUITY IS ";P-D
720   PRINT "FIRM MARGIN EXCESS IS ";P-D-P*.5
730   PRINT "BUYING POWER IS ";2*(P-D-P*.5)
740   PRINT "LEVEL WHERE EQUITY REQUIRED ";D/.7
750   PRINT "PERCENTAGE CHANGE FROM CURRENT LEVEL
      ";(P-D/.7)/P*100
```

PROGRAM 6–1   Compound Interest

```
10   PRINT "PRESENT VALUE OR PRINCIPAL IS "
20   INPUT P
30   PRINT "NUMBER OF YEARS FOR INVESTMENT"
40   INPUT N
50   PRINT "ANNUAL PERCENTAGE RATE OF INTEREST"
60   INPUT R
70   LET R=R/100
```

Compound Interest (*continued*)

```
 80   PRINT "NUMBER OF TIMES COMPOUNDED EACH YEAR"
 90   INPUT T
100   LET C = N*T
110   LET K = R/T
120   LET Q = (1 + K)[C
130   PRINT "FUTURE VALUE USING COMPOUND INTEREST IS
      ";P*Q
140   GOTO 10
```

PROGRAM 6-2   Present Value of Zero-Coupon Bond

```
 10   PRINT "FUTURE VALUE OR PAR IS "
 20   INPUT F
 30   PRINT "NUMBER OF YEARS FOR INVESTMENT"
 40   INPUT N
 50   PRINT "ANNUAL PERCENTAGE RATE OF INTEREST"
 60   INPUT R
 70   LET R = R/100
 80   PRINT "NUMBER OF TIMES COMPOUNDED EACH YEAR"
 90   INPUT T
100   LET C = N*T
110   LET K = R/T
120   LET Q = (1 + K)[C
130   PRINT "PRESENT VALUE OF ZERO COUPON BOND IS ";F/Q
140   GOTO 10
```

PROGRAM 6-3   Present Value of Coupon Bond

```
 10   PRINT "FUTURE VALUE OR PAR IS "
 15   INPUT F
 20   PRINT "COUPON AMOUNT RECEIVED EACH PERIOD"
 25   INPUT D
 30   PRINT "NUMBER OF YEARS FOR INVESTMENT"
 40   INPUT N
 50   PRINT "ANNUAL PERCENTAGE RATE OF INTEREST"
 60   INPUT R
 70   LET R = R/100
 80   PRINT "NUMBER OF TIMES COMPOUNDED EACH YEAR"
 90   INPUT T
100   LET C = N*T
```

Present Value of Coupon Bond (*continued*)

```
102   LET K=R/T
104   LET Q=(1+K)[C
115   LET S=0
120   LET J=0
121   LET J=J+1
126   LET Z=(1+K)[J
128   LET S=S+D/Z
129   IF J<C THEN GOTO 121
130   PRINT "PRESENT VALUE OF COUPON BOND IS ";F/Q+S
140   GOTO 10
```

PROGRAM 6–4   Annuity/Amortization Payment

```
10    PRINT "PRESENT VALUE OR PRINCIPAL IS "
20    INPUT P
30    PRINT "NUMBER OF YEARS FOR INVESTMENT"
40    INPUT N
50    PRINT "ANNUAL PERCENTAGE RATE OF INTEREST"
60    INPUT R
70    LET R=R/100
80    PRINT "NUMBER OF PAYMENTS EACH YEAR"
90    INPUT T
100   LET C=N*T
110   LET K=R/T
120   LET Q=(1+K)[C
130   PRINT "PERIOD PAYMENT BY ANNUITY ";P*K*Q/(Q−1)
140   GOTO 10
```

PROGRAM 6–5   Sinking Fund/IRA

```
6     PRINT "NUMBER OF DEPOSITS MADE EACH YEAR"
8     INPUT U
10    PRINT "AMOUNT DEPOSITED EACH PERIOD"
20    INPUT D
30    PRINT "NUMBER OF YEARS FOR INVESTMENT"
40    INPUT N
50    PRINT "ANNUAL PERCENTAGE RATE OF INTEREST"
60    INPUT R
70    LET R=R/100
80    PRINT "NUMBER OF TIMES COMPOUNDED EACH YEAR"
```

Sinking Fund/IRA (*continued*)

```
 90  INPUT T
100  LET C=N*T
110  LET K=R/T
112  LET P=D
114  LET L=INT(T/U)
118  LET J=0
119  LET Q=1
120  LET I=0
122  LET J=J+1
124  LET I=I+1
126  LET Q=Q*(1+K)
127  IF I=C THEN GOTO 130
128  IF J=L THEN GOTO 200
129  GOTO 122
130  PRINT "FUTURE VALUE OF SINKING FUND IS ";P*Q
132  GOTO 6
200  LET P=D+P*Q
210  LET Q=1
220  LET J=0
230  GOTO 122
```

PROGRAM 6–6   Interest Rate from Present and Future Values

```
 10  PRINT "PRESENT VALUE OR PRINCIPAL IS "
 20  INPUT P
 30  PRINT "NUMBER OF YEARS FOR INVESTMENT"
 40  INPUT N
 50  PRINT "FUTURE VALUE OR PAR IS "
 60  INPUT F
 70  LET R=R/100
 80  PRINT "NUMBER OF TIMES COMPOUNDED EACH YEAR"
 90  INPUT T
100  LET C=N*T
110  LET K=(F/P)[(1/C)-1
120  LET K=T*K*100
130  PRINT "INTEREST RATE IS ";K
140  GOTO 10
```

PROGRAM 6–7 Yield-to-Maturity

```
10   PRINT "FUTURE VALUE OR PAR IS "
20   INPUT F
30   PRINT "NUMBER OF YEARS TO BE INVESTED"
40   INPUT N
50   PRINT "COUPON AMOUNT RECEIVED EACH PERIOD"
60   INPUT D
70   PRINT "MARKET VALUE OF SECURITY"
80   INPUT M
90   LET Y = ((F − M)/N + D∗2)/((F + M)/2)
100  PRINT "YIELD-TO-MATURITY PERCENTAGE IS ";Y∗100
110  GOTO 10
```

PROGRAM 6–8 Yield-to-Call

```
10   PRINT "FUTURE VALUE OR PAR IS "
20   INPUT F
50   PRINT "COUPON AMOUNT RECEIVED EACH PERIOD"
60   INPUT D
70   PRINT "MARKET VALUE OF SECURITY"
80   INPUT M
90   PRINT "CALL PRICE OF BOND"
100  INPUT X
110  PRINT "NUMBER OF YEARS UNTIL BOND IS CALLABLE"
120  INPUT N
130  LET D = F/X∗D
140  LET M = F/X∗M
150  LET Y = ((F − M)/N + D∗2)/((F + M)/2)
160  PRINT "YIELD-TO-CALL PERCENTAGE IS ";Y∗100
170  GOTO 10
```

PROGRAM 6–9 Tax Planning

```
0    REM TABLE IS 1985 ESTIMATED TAX FOR JOINT RETURN—
     REPLACE AS NEEDED
1    DATA 169020,65151.70,50
2    DATA 113860,38123.30,49
3    DATA  89090,26976.80,45
4    DATA  62450,15788.00,42
5    DATA  47670,10171.60,38
```

Tax Planning (*continued*)

```
  6  DATA  36630,  6528.40,33
  7  DATA  31120,  4985.60,28
  8  DATA  25600,  3605.60,25
  9  DATA  21020,  2598.00,22
 10  DATA  16650,  1811.40,18
 11  DATA  12390,  1129.80,16
 12  DATA   7910,   502.60,14
 13  DATA   5720,   239.80,12
 14  DATA   3540,     0.00,11
 15  DATA      0,     0.00,0
 16  DATA      0,     0.00,0
 20  LET X=3540
 30  RESTORE
 40  PRINT "ENTER ADJUSTED GROSS INCOME"
 50  INPUT T
 60  PRINT "ENTER AMOUNT OF ITEMIZED DEDUCTIONS"
 70  INPUT D
 80  LET D=D-X
 90  IF D<0 THEN GOTO 110
100  LET T=T-D
110  PRINT "ENTER NUMBER OF EXEMPTIONS"
120  INPUT E
130  LET T=T-E*1040
140  IF D>0 THEN GOTO 180
150  PRINT "ENTER CHARITABLE CONTRIBUTION—SEE
     INSTRUCTIONS"
160  INPUT C
170  LET T=T-C
180  PRINT "TAXABLE INCOME IS ";T
190  LET I=0
200  LET I=I+1
210  READ A,B,C
220  IF T<A THEN GOTO 250
230  LET T=B+(T-A)*C/100
240  GOTO 260
250  IF I<16 THEN GOTO 200
260  PRINT "TAX IS ";T;"BRACKET IS ";C
270  PRINT "PRESS ENTER TO CONTINUE"
280  INPUT A$
290  GOTO 30
```

PROGRAM 6–10 Schedule D

```
 10   LET S=0
 20   PRINT "ENTER SHORT TERM GAINS OR LOSSES—ONE AT A
      TIME"
 30   LET T=0
 40   PRINT "IDENTIFY OR DESCRIBE PROPERTY"
 50   INPUT A$
 60   PRINT "PRICE RECEIVED AFTER COMMISSIONS"
 70   INPUT G
 80   PRINT "PROPERTY COST—INCLUDING COMMISSIONS"
 90   INPUT C
100   LET T=T+(G−C)
110   PRINT "NET PROFIT/LOSS IS ";G−C
120   PRINT "ENTER 999, WHEN FINISHED WITH SHORT TERM
      TRADES—0 OTHERWISE"
130   INPUT K
140   IF K<>999 THEN GOTO 40
150   PRINT "SHORT TERM NET IS ";T
160   PRINT "ENTER ANY SHORT TERM LOSS CARRYOVER"
170   INPUT L
175   LET T=T−L
180   PRINT "NET SHORT TERM GAIN OR LOSS IS ";T
190   PRINT "ENTER LONG TERM GAINS OR LOSSES—ONE AT A
      TIME"
200   PRINT "IDENTIFY/DESCRIBE PROPERTY"
210   INPUT A$
220   PRINT "PRICE RECEIVED AFTER COMMISSIONS"
230   INPUT G
240   PRINT "PROPERTY COST INCLUDING COMMISSIONS"
250   INPUT C
260   LET S=S+(G−C)
270   PRINT "NET PROFIT/LOSS IS ";G−C
280   PRINT "ENTER 888, IF FINISHED WITH LONG TERM
      TRADES—0 OTHERWISE"
290   INPUT K
300   IF K<>888 THEN GOTO 200
310   PRINT "LONG TERM NET IS ";S
320   PRINT "ENTER ANY LONG TERM LOSS CARRYOVER"
330   INPUT L
335   LET S=S−L
340   PRINT "NET LONG TERM GAIN OR LOSS IS ";S
350   LET N=T+S
360   PRINT "NET GAIN OR LOSS IS ";N
```

Schedule D (*continued*)

```
370   IF N<0 THEN GOTO 440
380   LET Q=N
390   IF N>S THEN LET Q=S
400   IF S<=0 THEN LET Q=0
410   LET V=.60*Q
420   PRINT "TAXABLE CAPITAL GAIN IS ";N-V
430   GOTO 500
440   IF T>=0 THEN LET Q=.5*(T+S)
450   IF S>=0 THEN LET Q=T+S
460   IF (S<0)*(T<0) THEN LET Q=T+.5*S
470   LET R=3000
480   IF Q>R THEN LET Q=R
490   PRINT "MAXIMUM CAPITAL LOSS IS ";Q
500   LET V=0
510   IF T>0 THEN GOTO 580
520   IF S>0 THEN LET V=S+T
530   IF Q>V THEN LET Q=V
540   LET R=Q
550   PRINT "SHORT TERM LOSS CARRYOVER IS ";V-Q
560   LET Q=R-Q
570   LET V=0
580   IF S>0 THEN GOTO 610
590   IF T>0 THEN LET V=S+T
600   LET V=V-2*Q
610   PRINT "LONG TERM LOSS CARRYOVER IS ";V
```

PROGRAM 6–11 Full-Service and Discount Commissions

```
 1   DATA 400,10.,0.0,1.6,19
 2   DATA 1000,2.5,0.0,1.6,19
 3   DATA 2000,2.0,5.0,1.6,19
 4   DATA 2500,1.3,19.,1.6,19
 5   DATA 5000,1.3,19.,0.6,44
 6   DATA 6000,1.6,4.0,0.6,44
 7   DATA 10000,1.6,4.0,0.3,62
 8   DATA 22000,1.04,59,0.3,62
 9   DATA 30000,1.04,59,0.2,84
10   DATA 50000,.55,205,0.2,84
11   DATA 300000,.55,205,0.1,134
12   DATA 500000,.20,255,0.1,134
13   DATA 1000000,.20,255,.08,234
```

Full-Service and Discount Commissions (*continued*)

```
20   PRINT "ENTER NUMBER OF SHARES"
30   INPUT N
40   PRINT "ENTER PRICE PER SHARE"
50   INPUT P
60   RESTORE
70   LET T=N*P
80   READ W,X,Y,E,F
90   IF T>W THEN GOTO 80
100  LET C=T*X/100+Y
110  IF N<101 THEN LET C=C+12+.03*N
120  IF N>400 THEN LET C=C+40+.05*N
130  IF (N>100)*(N<401) THEN LET C=C+.15*N
140  IF (C<40)*(T>400) THEN LET C=40
150  LET Q=.97*N
160  IF (N>100)*(C>Q) THEN LET C=Q
170  LET D=C/T*100
180  PRINT "ESTIMATED COMMISSIONS BASED ON JULY 1985
     RATES"
190  PRINT "FULL SERVICE COMMISSION IS ";C;"FOR ";D;"
     PERCENT"
200  LET C=T*E/100+F
210  IF N<900 THEN LET Q=.08*N
220  IF N>899 THEN LET Q=.04*(N-900)+72
230  IF Q>C THEN LET C=Q
240  IF (N<101)*(C>49) THEN LET C=49
250  IF N>100 THEN LET Q=.45*(N-100)+49
260  LET Q=10000
270  IF Q<C THEN LET C=Q
280  IF C<34 THEN LET C=34
300  LET D=C/T*100
310  PRINT "DISCOUNT COMMISSION IS ";C;" FOR";D;"
     PERCENT"
320  GOTO 20
```

Substitutions

Descriptive Statistics (3–3)

Where a computer doesn't have the exponential operator ([↑ ^ or **), replace statement 260 with:

260 PRINT "STANDARD DEVIATION IS "; SQR(Z/P − 1))

If your machine can't handle SQR, then replace statements 260 and 270 with the following sequence:

260 LET X = Z/(P − 1)
270 LET Y = .5*X
280 LET Z = 0
290 LET W = (X/Y − Y)*.5
300 IF (W = 0) + (W = Z) THEN GOTO 340
310 LET Y = Y + W
320 LET Z = W
330 GOTO 290
340 PRINT "STANDARD DEVIATION IS ";Y
350 GOTO 20

Compound Interest (6–1), Present Value of Zero-Coupon Bond (6–2), Annuity/Amortization Payment (6–4)

To substitute for the exponential operator, replace statement 120 with:

120 LET Q = 1
122 LET I = 0
124 LET I = I + 1

```
126  LET Q=Q*(1+K)
128  IF I<C THEN GOTO 124
```

Present Value of a Bond (6–3)

To correct for no exponential operator, replace statement 126 with:

```
122  LET Z=1
124  LET I=0
125  LET I=I+1
126  LET Z=Z*(1+K)
127  IF I<J THEN GOTO 125
```

Replace statement 104 with:

```
104  LET Q=1
106  LET I=0
108  LET I=I+1
110  LET Q=Q*(1+K)
112  IF I<C THEN GOTO 108
```

Annuity/Amortization Payment (6–4)

Depending on your choice of an annuity to be paid to you or amortization to be paid on a mortgage, use one of the following statements:

```
130  PRINT "PERIOD PAYMENT BY ANNUITY
     ";P*K*Q/(Q-1)
130  PRINT "AMORTIZATION PAYMENT IS
     ";P*K*Q/(Q-1)
```

Sinking Fund/IRA (6–5)

If the INT function cannot be handled by your computer, replace line 114 with the following sequence:

```
113  LET E=T/U
114  IF E<1 THEN GOTO 117
115  LET E=E-1
116  GOTO 114
117  LET L=T/U-E
```

Recommended Reading List

1. CROWELL, RICHARD A. *Stock Market Strategy.* New York: McGraw-Hill, 1977.

2. DREMAN, DAVID. *The New Contrarian Investment Strategy.* New York: Random House, 1982.

3. ENGEL, LOUIS. *How to Buy Stocks.* New York: Bantam Books, 1981.

4. GRAHAM, BENJAMIN. *The Intelligent Investor.* New York: Harper & Row, 1965.

5. HAGIN, ROBERT. *Modern Portfolio Theory.* Homewood, Ill.: Dow Jones-Irwin, 1979.

6. LITTLE, JEFFREY B., and LUCIEN RHODES. *Understanding Wall Street.* Cockeysville, Md.: Liberty Publishing, 1980.

7. MALKIEL, BURTON G. *A Random Walk down Wall Street.* New York: W. W. Norton, 1981.

8. RILEY, WILLIAM B., JR., and AUSTIN H. MONTGOMERY, JR. *Guide to Computer-Assisted Investment Analysis.* New York: McGraw-Hill, 1982.

Glossary

Absolute deviation   The difference between an individual value and the mean of the data.

Academic   A person who believes in totally efficient markets.

Amortization   Payment of a lump sum and interest over a set schedule.

Annual earnings-per-share   See earnings.

Annual meeting   Once-a-year business meeting conducted with stockholders.

Annual rate-of-return   See return.

Annual report   Once-a-year report by management to stockholders.

Annuity   Distribution of a lump sum and interest over a set schedule of payments.

Asked   Price sought by holder of stock. See bid.

Assets   Everything a company owns (money, property, inventory, etc.).

At-the-market   An order to buy or sell at the best price currently available.

Averaging down   Making additional investment in a declining market.

Averaging up   Making additional investment in a rising market.

Balance sheet   A financial statement showing assets and liabilities.

Bankruptcy A state of insolvency, where assets are exceeded by liabilities.

BASIC Beginners All-purpose Symbolic Instruction Code—a programming language.

Bear market A falling market.

Beta The market risk of a stock found by relating percentage change of a stock to an index.

Bid Buyers price offer for a stock.

Bonds A promise to pay a stated rate of interest for a defined period and to return the principal at maturity.

Book value Assets, less liabilities, divided by the number of common shares.

Broker An agent to buy and sell stocks for a commission.

Bucket shop A gambling house, now outlawed, that allowed bets to be placed on stock movement.

Bull market A rising market.

Call Provision for redemption of bond by debtor before maturity date. Also the option to buy a stock at a given price by a certain date.

Capital Money for expansion of company.

Capital asset Securities, properties, commodities, options, etc. No futures.

Capital gain Profit from the sale of a capital asset.

Capital loss Loss from the sale of a capital asset.

Chapter Eleven The section of the bankruptcy code that provides protection from creditors.

Charting Recording of price and volume data on two-dimensional graphs.

Commission The fee paid a broker to transfer a stock from a seller to a buyer.

Common stock Ownership of a company denoted in shares.

Computer An electro-mechanical device that can perform arithmetical/logical operations from a stored sequence of instructions.

Constant A number used by a computer that can't be changed.

Correlation The degree to which two variables are related.

Cost of sales Expenses associated with the sale of a company's product.

Current assets Assets that are readily transformed into cash.

Current liabilities Obligations that must paid immediately.

Current ratio Current assets divided by current liabilities.

Data Information represented as numbers and alphabetical characters.

Database A large collection of data.

Day order Order, to be canceled if not executed by the end of the current trading day.

Day trading Buying and selling the stock in the same day (once had favorable margin provisions).

Disc A phonograph-like recording medium for computer data.

Diversification Dividing your money between two or more securities.

Dividend Sharing of profits with stockholders.

Dollar-cost-averaging Putting fixed amounts into stocks at regular intervals.

Dow-Jones Industrials Average (DJIA) An index of 30 leading stocks of the New York Stock Exchange useful for historical perspective.

Earnings Net income of company after expenses—usually expressed in dollars per share of common stock.

Earnings yield Annual earnings per share of a company divided by the market price per share.

Equity Original investment, plus retained assets, less liabilities.

Exponential A relationship between two variables where a change in one causes a disproportionate change in the other.

Filters   The placement of stop orders in a systematic fashion.

Fixed income   Securities with a dividend that is fixed for the life of the security.

Fixed unit   A change in stock price that is a set number rather than a percentage.

Fundamental analysis   Analysis by factors such as sales, earnings, and assets.

Fundamentalist   A person who believes in fundamental analysis to select stocks.

Futures   A contract to buy or sell a commodity by some future date at a price set now.

Graphics   On computers, the display of information in pictorial form.

Growth   Numerical improvement in price or earnings.

Hedge   To reduce risk (and return) by making some investment that will work counter to the principal portfolio.

Individual Retirement Account (IRA)   A government sponsored investment plan where taxation is deferred until funds are removed.

Inflation   The annual percentage change in the Consumer Price Index (CPI).

Intangibles   Company assets that are other than physical. This could include patents, copyrights, goodwill.

Interest rates   The annual percentage of principal that is to be paid for use of the principal.

Investing   To buy properties with the anticipation of principal growth through capital gains and interest.

Keough   A government sponsored investment plan for businesses similar to the IRA for individuals

Leverage   Use of borrowed funds to increase holdings.

Liabilities   Everything a company owes (loans, accounts payable, etc.).

Limit move   In commodity trading, the maximum amount a price may vary from day-to-day.

Limit order   Offering to buy or sell a property at a specific price.

Linear   A relationship between two variables, where a change in one produces a proportional change in the other.

Liquidation   The sale or disposal of assets.

Long term   The period of time required by law for favorable taxation of capital gains. Currently six months and a day, but subject to change by Congress.

Margin   The use of the broker's money to buy securities.

Margin calls   Requirement from broker for more equity in the account.

Margin maintenance   Adding funds to the account to raise equity in a portfolio losing value.

Market letter   A periodical advising subscribers on market direction and expected stock performance.

Market order   Offer to buy or sell as soon as possible at prevailing price.

Market price   The price of a security where someone is willing to buy when another is willing to sell.

Mathematical expectation   The estimated return from a game (or investment) after a systematic number of trials.

Mean   The sum of all elements in a population divided by the number of elements.

Model   A mathematical simplification and simulation of reality.

Modern Portfolio Theory (MPT)   The use of mathematical statistics to select stocks and manage portfolios.

Moving average   The mean value of a subset of points taken from a time series. As new points are produced, a new average (mean) is computed, adding to a time series of averages.

Mutual funds   An investment trust that sells shares of its portfolio.

Net sales   Revenue received by a company after allowing for returns and reductions.

New issue   First sale of stock to the public.

No-load   No initial mutual fund commission.

Odd-lot   Less than 100 shares of a stock.

Open order   Limit or stop order unexecuted but still active.

Operating expenses   Corporate expenses including cost of goods sold, depreciation, and selling and administrative expenses.

Operating system   A master control program in constant use on a computer performing logistical services to a user program.

Operations report (10K)   A detailed statement of company business and problems, including all litigation, required by the SEC.

Option   The right to buy or sell stock at a predetermined price by a preset date. See put, call.

Ordinary income   Under the tax law, all salaried and investment income that doesn't qualify for capital gains treatment.

Over-the-counter   Unlisted stocks bought directly from brokers.

Par value   Face or original value of security.

Percentage   Difference from an original value divided by the value and multiplied by 100.

Perpetual   A type of bond that is indefinite—no maturity date.

Personal computer   A small desktop computer usually consisting of keyboard and logic. Must have a monitor or printer to be useful. Tape or disc storage units are desirable.

Pink sheets   Quotations on small companies rarely traded.

Point and figure   A charting method concerned only with major movements in price.

Portfolio   An itemized list of current investments.

Positioning   The process of buying an investment.

Preferred stock   Stock with rights that take preference over common shares.

Price-earnings ratio   Price of stock divided by annual earnings per share.

Principal   The basic value of the initial investment.

Program   A sequence of computer instructions.

Prospectus Essential facts on a company distributed prior to stock offering.

Put The option to sell a stock at a given price by a certain date.

Pyramiding The process of adding to an investment position as the price increases.

Quick ratio Current assets less inventories, divided by current liabilities.

Random walk Unpredictable movement in stock prices in amplitude and direction.

Real rate of return Return on an investment after deducting the inflation rate and any risk factors.

Regression The formulated relationship of two or more variables.

Return The expected reward from an investment stated in an average annual percentage.

Risk The potential loss from an investment due to change in price and/or dividend.

Screens Well defined conditions that are used for a systematic search of a database.

Securities Stocks and bonds in all varied forms.

Securities and Exchange Commission (SEC) A commission set by Congress to regulate and provide information on publicly held companies.

Share Part of the company.

Short selling To sell borrowed stock with the intent of buying a replacement at lower prices.

Short-against-the-box Selling your own stock short and delaying delivery until a new tax year begins.

Short term Investments not held long enough to qualify for long term capital gains treatment.

Sinking fund An investment created by systematic deposits without withdrawal.

Speculation Buying properties in anticipation of significant increase in value.

Spread The difference between bid and asked prices. Also a put and call on the same stock for the same period.

Spread sheet An accounting of money transactions in tabular form.

Square root A number that multiplied by itself gives the starting value. Four is the square root of sixteen.

Standard deviation The square root of the variance.

Stock See common stock.

Stop orders An offer to buy or sell if price returns to some prior level. A method of protecting against significant loss.

Storage A logical unit of the computer that provides preservation of information.

Straddle A put and call on the same stock for the same period at the same striking price.

Strap A straddle with two calls and one put.

Striking price The price specified in the option.

Strip A straddle with two puts and one call.

Tape The record of stock transactions as they occur. Also a storage medium for computer information.

Taxes A percentage of one's income or wealth paid to support government.

Tax bracket The position in a tax table, indicating the percentage of additional dollars earned that must go to taxes.

Technical analysis A theory of investing on the basis of recent price and volume action in the market.

Technician A person that uses technical analysis.

Tick An increase or decrease in price from last trade. Usually ⅛ on stocks.

Ticker A coded tape of all stock transactions as they occur.

Time series Data collected regularly over a period of time.

Trading Buying and selling of securities after very short holding periods.

Transaction   The transfer of a security from seller to buyer.

Underwriter   A brokerage firm guaranteeing and handling the sale of a new issue.

Unit change   A fixed dollar amount of price change. Contrast with percentage change.

Value   Judgment of worth not necessarily confirmed by market participants.

Value Line Investment Survey   A stock market data service.

Variable   Use of symbolism to represent changing values.

Variance   The sum of the squared differences between each item in a population and the population mean divided by the total number of elements in the population.

Vector   Pictorial or graphical representation of amplitude and direction of force.

Volatility   A measure of the relative magnitude of price variation represented as beta.

Volume   Total number of shares transacted (transferred).

Warrants   A call option issued by the company.

Word processing   The manipulation and editing of textual material electronically.

Working capital   The net difference between current assets and current liabilities.

Yield   Annual dividend divided by principal and multiplied by 100.

Yield, coupon   Yield based on par value of investment.

Yield, current   Yield based on market value of investment.

Yield-to-call   Yield with capital gains based on the average of current and call prices.

Yield-to-maturity   Yield with capital gains based on the average of current and par prices.

Zero coupon   A bond paying all interest due with the return of principal at maturity.

Index